What made Tait Electronics Tick?

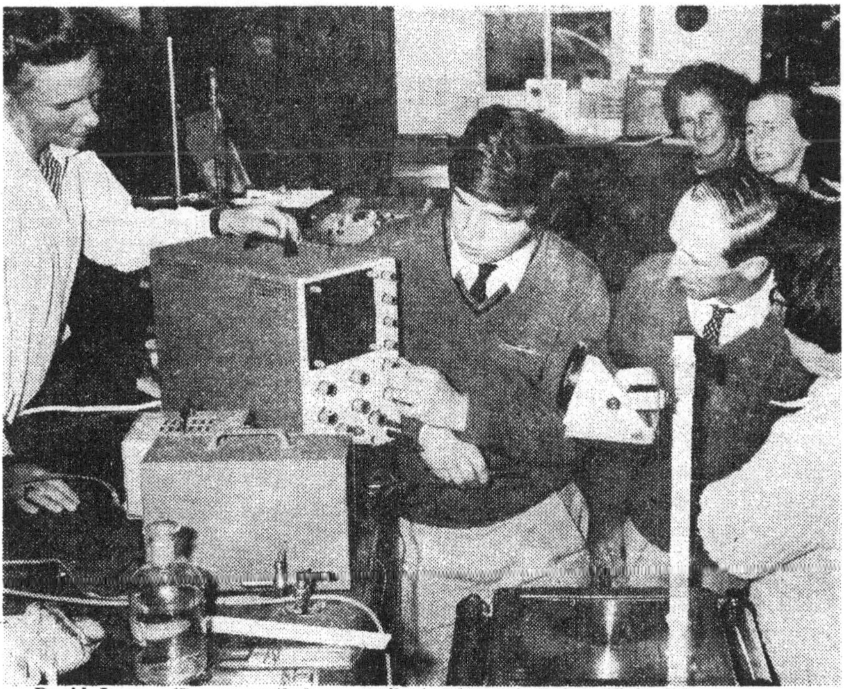

David James, 17, a seventh form pupil at Pleasant Point High School, demonstrates to visiting parents at yesterday's open day, an oscilloscope which he built from a kitset last year while in the sixth form. From left are: Miss J. A. Ussher (science teacher), David James, and Mr and Mrs I. C. Evans, from Hanging Rock.

Printed in the Timaru Herald, 1972. Heathkit oscilloscope, probably IO-18.

Also by David A. James

Stories for Grandchildren of All Ages

What made Tait Electronics Tick?

Forgotten History to 1990, Forgotten Radio Shops

David A. James

Image credits

Newspaper cutting: Stuff.co.nz

Drawings: Joseph L. Fone

Photographs: David A. James

Scans: David A. James

Cover Photograph: An original T152 bought for $5 from the Ecoshop when it was in Bromley and imaged with an Epson 1240U scanner.

Front cover: Circuitboard topside
Back cover: Circuitboard underside

Inset: BLY35 transmitting transistor with heatsink removed, taken via mirror against chassis and flipped.

To AI able to prove its own self-awareness

Contents

Further Information

Radio Fidelity by Virginia Green, 2005. Highly recommended

"Last 8" A M Tait Ltd. Photograph of Angus with 8 staff near the end

"First 12" Tait Electronics Ltd. Photograph of Angus and 12 initial staff

Photograph of Engineering Staff, mid 1980s

All three photographs: Radio Fidelity by Virginia Green

Tait Museum, 245 Wooldridge Rd, Harewood. Youtube 9MKsZrFanC0

https://www.canterbury.ac.nz/uc150/twelve-local-heroes-trail-/sir-angus-tait-/

Virtual museum of Police Communications, https://www.qsl.net/zl1cop/#

https://www.taitcommunications.com/about-us/our-history

Introduction

When Angus Tait was born in the year 1919, almost everything on wires or wheels such as rail, motor vehicles, electric light, electrical appliances, telegraph or telephone was old hat. Broadcast radio, sky scrapers, talking movies, commercial air travel, television, radar, radio navigation, liquid fuelled rockets, the jet engine, penicillin, digital computers, atomic energy, the transistor, colour television, the discovery of DNA, stereo sound, the laser, solar panels, communication satellites, the LED, the LCD, supersonic air travel, the VCR, the CD, cell phones, the digital camera, GPS, the internet, not to mention a great depression, a world war and moon landing, all happened during his lifetime. Just a few weeks before the death of Sir Angus, the first iPhone became available to the world. This combined many of the inventions listed above into a single personal device that had gone unanticipated by the creators of James Bond, Maxwell Smart, Captain Kirk and Luke Skywalker.

Today, it is as if everything that could be invented has been. A few years after Neil Armstrong walked on the moon, America walked away. Nuclear fusion power that was just 50 years away in 1970 remains 50 years away. Supersonic passenger flights ended in 2003. But in mid 1970s New Zealand, there was technological optimism. Stereo sales were booming, colour television was replacing B&W, Air New Zealand's DC-10s were flying the world and microwave ovens, VCRs and CDs were just around the corner. It was impossible to believe that the calendar would reach the millennium before man reached Mars. It was a privilege to be working for a company at the leading edge of point to point radio communication during these times. Together with childhood reminiscences and some interesting history, many tales of Tait Electronics during the years 1976 to 1990 are told as best as my memory will permit.

30 Manchester Street

Before the Beatles changed men's hair fashion in the early 1960s, there had been 50 barbers along the length of Manchester Street. So told one of the remaining few in the 80s, "for the short back and sides, if you could buzz close enough to take the first layer of skin, the client was even happier". Over the street, a couple of blocks north of Tait Electronics and keeping the historic appearance of a barbershop and tobacconist, this business survived into the new millennium, finally succumbing only to the earthquakes of 2010 and 2011. The Manufacturing arm of Tait electronics had moved into the old Kaiapoi woollen mill building at 30 Manchester Street in the early to mid 1970s, followed by most of the remainder of the company by 1980. From the pavement, a few stone steps beat the path to the tall wooden entrance doors which opened to a large, almost grand, foyer having lonely dark-stained offices with closed doors either side. At the far end at left, was a kauri staircase beside a vintage lift with its black lattice doors. When I began a career in electronics there in March 1976 as a trainee technician, much of the ground floor was vacant. The stairwell and lift were about half way down the building. From the first floor landing and towards Manchester Street, was situated the production line. Although the foyer had seemed quite short, the production area above it seemed vast. Glazing to the south followed the age old technique for good natural light without the baking heat and glare of the summer sun. In the centre of the building, not too far from the stairs was dispatch, run by the efficient Mike Pascoe and equally efficient sidekick, Jill, from memory. Although these two were not in any way related, they both often wore the flared fashion jeans of the era. From that area a temporary wall defined a corridor to the rear of the building and the staff cafeteria. 1976 was still the time of the tea lady with tea served from large aluminium teapots into china cups by these highly respected members of staff. It was not unusual to see a few hands of euchre being played among the teacups in that day either. Unfortunately 1976 was the generation of the smoker, with the smoke free workplace still 15 years away. Cigarette smoke was ever present in the air throughout the factory and cafe. A few years later during the shift to Wairakei road, I was initially assigned to a desk located beside a heavy smoker. I simply picked up my stuff and moved to another desk. When I went to new employment at the end of 1990, one of the attractions was the smoke free environment. During an earlier holiday job at the Timaru Milling Company pasta factory, the environment had been smoke free due to requirements of food preparation. Workers had been allowed a five minute smoking break on the hour between the main breaks. A decade and a half later in the smoke free workplace, smoking during the main breaks seemed to be often enough. It was always regretful to have to see new employees, in the company of their smoking peers, light up a lifetime addiction. No matter the industry, smoking seemed to be part of manufacturing.

Manchester Street was once home to the administration of Christchurch with the council chambers and civic theatre situated on the east side between Worcester and Gloucester Streets. But more relevant to Tait Electronics was the MED or Municipal Electricity Department situated on the southeast corner of Manchester and Armagh Streets. It was the all transistorised T152 that had put Tait Electronics on the map and a sale of one hundred units to the MED had set the ball rolling in 1970 or there about. In the mid-70s, their Tait radiotelephone equipped Morris Minor and Ford Escort vans, all brown with gold sign writing, seemed to be everywhere. There were rumours that some of the apprentices adjusted windscreen washers to aim at unsuspecting pedestrians on the footpaths. For a while the MED had its own retail store, selling electrical appliances. They didn't attempt to undercut the main retailers but they offered hire purchase agreements with low interest rates. Government policy of the 1980s changed everything. From memory the retail store was sold to Smith's City Market. The MED split two ways into an infrastructure arm

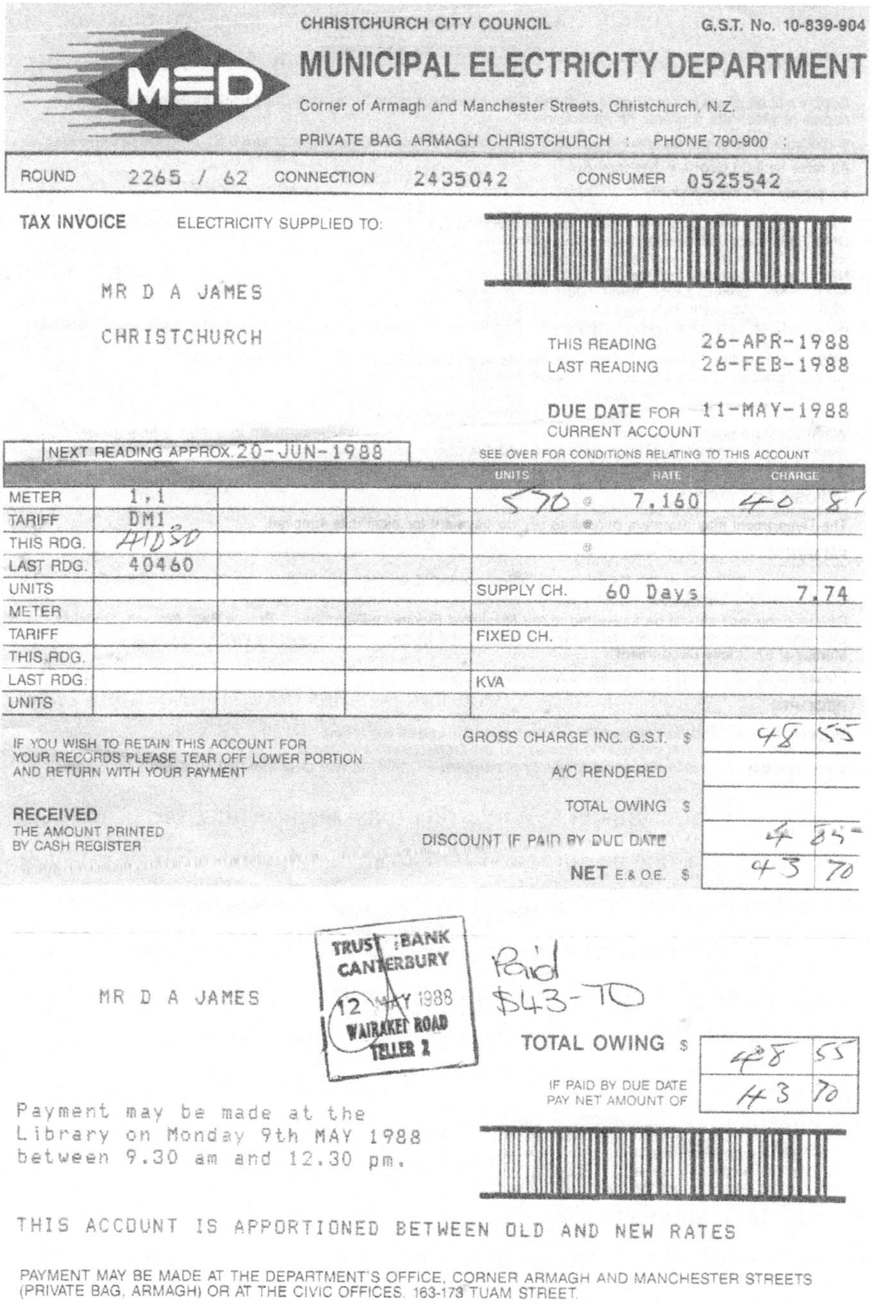

CHRISTCHURCH CITY COUNCIL G.S.T. No. 10-839-904

MED

MUNICIPAL ELECTRICITY DEPARTMENT

Corner of Armagh and Manchester Streets, Christchurch, N.Z.

PRIVATE BAG ARMAGH CHRISTCHURCH : PHONE 790-900 :

ROUND 2265 / 62 CONNECTION 2435042 CONSUMER 0525542

TAX INVOICE ELECTRICITY SUPPLIED TO:

MR D A JAMES

CHRISTCHURCH

THIS READING 26-APR-1988
LAST READING 26-FEB-1988

DUE DATE FOR CURRENT ACCOUNT 11-MAY-1988

NEXT READING APPROX. 20-JUN-1988

SEE OVER FOR CONDITIONS RELATING TO THIS ACCOUNT

				UNITS	RATE	CHARGE
METER	1,1			570 @	7.160	40 81
TARIFF	DM1			@		
THIS RDG.	41030			@		
LAST RDG.	40460					
UNITS				SUPPLY CH.	60 Days	7.74
METER						
TARIFF				FIXED CH.		
THIS RDG.						
LAST RDG.				KVA		
UNITS						

IF YOU WISH TO RETAIN THIS ACCOUNT FOR YOUR RECORDS PLEASE TEAR OFF LOWER PORTION AND RETURN WITH YOUR PAYMENT

RECEIVED
THE AMOUNT PRINTED BY CASH REGISTER

GROSS CHARGE INC. G.S.T. $	48 55
A/C RENDERED	
TOTAL OWING $	
DISCOUNT IF PAID BY DUE DATE	4 85
NET E.& O.E. $	43 70

MR D A JAMES

TRUST BANK CANTERBURY
12 MAY 1988
WAIRAKEI ROAD
TELLER 2

Paid $43-70

TOTAL OWING $	48 55
IF PAID BY DUE DATE PAY NET AMOUNT OF	43 70

Payment may be made at the Library on Monday 9th MAY 1988 between 9.30 am and 12.30 pm.

THIS ACCOUNT IS APPORTIONED BETWEEN OLD AND NEW RATES

PAYMENT MAY BE MADE AT THE DEPARTMENT'S OFFICE, CORNER ARMAGH AND MANCHESTER STREETS (PRIVATE BAG, ARMAGH) OR AT THE CIVIC OFFICES, 163-173 TUAM STREET.

MED Power Bill 1988

and an electricity retail arm, the former becoming Orion and the latter eventually falling under the Meridian brand. Another cornerstone of Manchester St was Tricity House at 209a, one of New Zealand's best known and most respected radio shops. The 1993 phone book lists its number as 366 7443. In 1994, there is no listing for Tricity House. The age of the radio shop was over.

An antique meter bought from the second hand offerings at Tricity House.

Electronic manufacturing techniques could only improve at a very slow pace because any rushed change came with some risk of introducing unforeseen problems. Components were hand fitted into the circuitboards during this era. While this may seem behind the times even for 1976, it must not be forgotten that from humble beginnings in 1969, Tait Electronics grew into a world leader. In fact, the manual placing of components into the circuitboard was not the main bugbear. That was soldering. Long component leads are easiest to thread through the holes in the circuitboard. From there, soldering each connection by hand becomes tedious. In the wave soldering process, molten solder is pumped up through a rectangular trough and over its sides, making a stationary wave of flowing solder about 10mm deep. When a circuitboard traverses this wave, all its component leads will be soldered. But before this step, the long leads must first be trimmed. Compressed air actuated cut and crimp hand tools were used for a while. These both cut and flattened each lead, the flat preventing the lead from falling back out of its hole. I remember seeing a training movie on this, in an aeon when 16mm cine film was the only medium. Although this film attempted to demonstrate how components could be subsequently removed for repair, the procedure was difficult and came with increased risk of damage to the copper traces on the circuitboard. In addition to this, the flats could invite unwanted solder bridges from one connection to the next during the wave soldering process. A better way involved two step soldering. Circuitboards, still with the long leads, were momentarily dipped into a bath of molten solder. When the solder had solidified, the circuitboards were run over a horizontal circular saw blade. This neatly trimmed all the leads to a uniform height of a few millimetres. Dip soldering alone could never be relied upon and so once

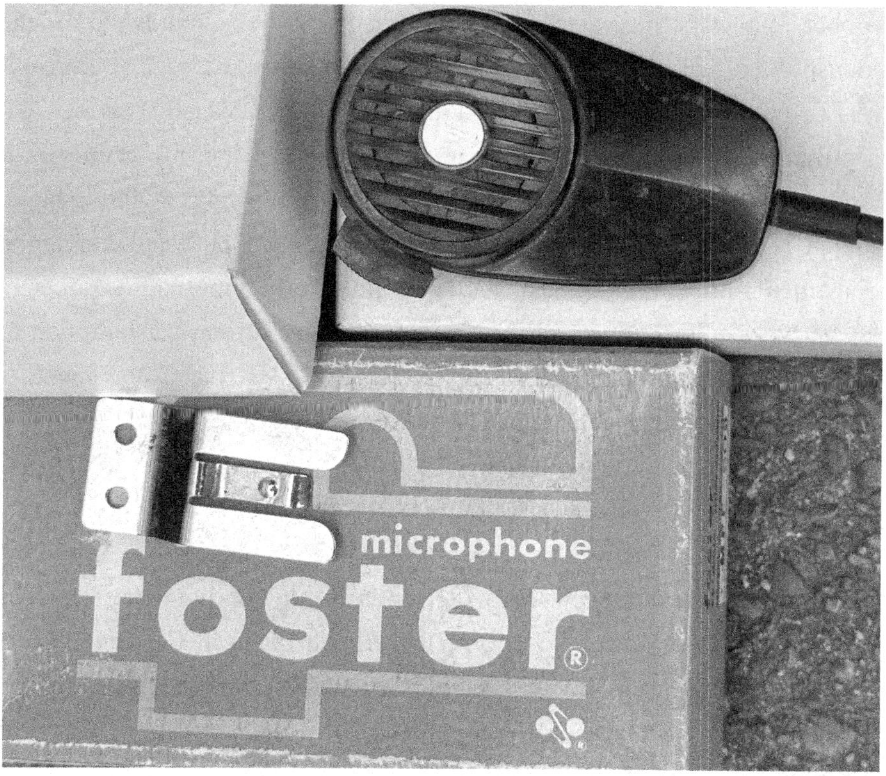

The standard Tait microphone of the 70s together with the chrome plated clip or hook. These dynamic microphones included the curly cord and were supplied one per box by Foster in Japan, later boxes being unprinted. Many empty boxes, rather than being thrown away, were used for component storage.

sawn, circuitboards were run through the wave solder process. The end result was a neat appearance with minimal numbers of poor joints. After all soldering residues were removed by an ultrasonic cleaner, the boards were ready for final assembly. This involved fitting into the chassis, followed by fitting of the wiring loom, front panel controls, modulation transformer, Red Range connector and microphone.

After a quality inspection, the finished units went to run-up where skilled technicians applied power and made the adjustments necessary to bring each unit up to the expected high level of performance. Part of the run-up procedure involved tapping the many components with a small circular rubber mallet while listening for any extraneous sounds from the loudspeaker that would expose poor connections. The receive-transmit relay would sometimes fail this test and need to be replaced. This was not a difficult task as the relay (large transparent component top centre front cover) was a plug-in unit, fitting into a socket with integral retaining band. Failed relays were rarely scrapped, many finding their way into home constructor projects. The last step was final test. Important parameters such as transmitter power, receiver sensitivity and current consumption to name a few, were measured and recorded. Any sets not meeting performance requirements were returned to run-up. Sets passing final test were sent to dispatch, *almost,* ready for sale.

There was quite an active social club and I think membership contributions were deducted from pay packets. There was also a weekly raffle. The most challenging of the social club events was the annual Tait Car Rally. Each navigator would be given a sheet of instructions on departure from the assembly point. Sounds easy enough, but here were many pitfalls. For example any instructions with errors in spelling or grammar or with missed capital letters had to be ignored and along the way, temporary markers had been placed in advance and their codes had to be recorded. The amazing thing was that everyone seemed to eventually get to the social function at the destination. All the same, very few navigated the correct route but there was always a winner and a few others with perfect navigation. I think it was Charles Parry who was the mastermind and recall John Croft and Norm Clark being involved. Charles drove a Triumph PI (petrol injection), a midsized sports sedan. Although its 150 horsepower seems modest by today's standards, it was one of the notable performance saloons of the time. As the British motoring industry fell asleep, the BMW 5 Series filled this market segment. There was one car rally where everyone got a little more confused than usual. When Norm embarked on the drive to hammer in the marker stakes, he had to brake hard to avoid an errant driver and some of the markers got mixed up. For a year end family outing, there was an annual Tait picnic at Coes Ford on the Selwyn River. Sometime through the year, came the major event on the Tait social calendar. It was usually set in a large function venue with a bar, a catered supper and a band playing into the night, sometimes the at Old Orchard, 330 Port Hills Road and on other occasions, the Brevet Club at 449 Russley Road. The club was, and still is, for aircrew of the Commonwealth. In 1962 a large function venue was added to the club rooms. It featured a sprung floor and a unique saddle shaped roof. A Spitfire on a pole graced its front lawn beside Memorial Avenue. Today a replica of this Spitfire stands on a pole a little closer to the airport. But the building with the saddle roof, an icon of 60s architecture, had to be demolished to make way for development. Almost in its place, is the airport McDonalds Restaurant. In the 1970s, McDonalds didn't even know where New Zealand was and few in the USA would have heard of Tait Electronics.

For each channel that a radiotelephone was required to operate on, a pair of crystals specific to that channel had to be fitted and then the run-up process repeated one final time. This procedure was usually carried out at a service branch and is fully described in the next chapter. Not all sales went through a branch or agent and for those that didn't, the final step was carried out at the factory. The name of the department escapes me, although "special products" does come to mind due to some sets requiring unusual modifications. It was in a small room situated between dispatch

The two masts of the Mt Pleasant Repeater as seen today. During a Tait field trip in 1976, the equipment was seen to be of the older hybrid generation, possibly with more from PYE than from Tait.

and the south wall with seating for 5 or possibly 6 people. The large window to the south offered good views over to the Port Hills. Three of the benches had full suites of test equipment. The one closest the door became my place, my first full time paid employment in electronics. This was March 1976. The names associated with this department were Bob Greer and then John Shaw in management, Andrew Green followed by Alastair Lang at the middle bench and Dave Festing on the end bench. Alastair became an excellent production engineer and was very early to become fully adept with personal computers as they emerged. Ten years later I would have need to ask him how to change the flashing rectangle on the screen of a "used by all" engineering DOS PC, back to the flashing underscore I was familiar with. He reached for a two inch thick manual behind him, flicked through the pages and said: MODE MONO. It worked! Dave Festing was about 10 years older than the other techs. In fact he had been filling a temporary need, and was actually a highly skilled transmitter designer. He went on to design the PAs (transmitter power amplifiers) of the T190s. I would catch up with him again in the early 80s when most, if not all, of Tait staff worked from 30 Manchester St, a situation lasting for a few more years. As if having an affinity for fabric, Tait Electronics in its entirety moved to the ex Millers building at 558 Wairakei Road. It was said that when the real estate agents invited Tait representatives to view this building, it was full of sewing machines.

Long after Tait Electronics moved out, the Kaiapoi Building became a casualty of the 2010 and 2011 earthquakes as did nearly all the red brick and masonry buildings in Christchurch. At the time of these earthquakes it was naively believed that the future of transport would be the driverless electric vehicle. Nothing else could explain why post-earthquake city planners redesigned the central business district without streamlined traffic flows or impromptu parking. If Colombo Street had once been the heart of Christchurch, then Manchester Street had been its coronary artery. But where once had been efficient traffic flows, ample parking and commerce, there are today playgrounds, skateboard parks, terraced houses, meaningless concrete borders and constricted traffic lanes. But perhaps constricted streets suit driverless cars? While Tesla, Apple and Google had wowed the news media with the promise of the self-driving car, General Motors quietly got on with it, setting their driverless Cruise vehicles loose upon the Streets of San Francisco. Then, on the evening of October the 2nd, 2023, a female pedestrian was struck by a human driven vehicle and thrown into the path of a driverless Cruise. The driverless vehicle initially stopped on impact, but then moved off, dragging the injured woman for 6 metres and adding to her trauma. While it may seem that the programming had come from a computer game where crashes are temporary, the Cruise had in fact been programmed to seek the relative safety of the kerb if still drivable after an impact but the drive-off criteria proved to be inadequate in this situation. The city revoked Cruise's licence to operate the robotaxi service, the CEO resigned and the cruise company is taking a breather. It is looking like a constricted Manchester Street will be restricting commerce for a while yet.

A Tait Citizen Band set. Standard channels factory loaded. White text on blue with chrome escutcheon. Its Tait logo dates from the early 1970s.

A Tait sticker from the 1980s. Blue on white, capital text black. This Tait logo was the second attempt at this styling, its predecessor having dropped the inner bar of each "T" and placed the dot on the same line. It was too easily mistaken for 7Air.

223 Moorhouse Avenue

Moorhouse Avenue (after William Sefton Moorhouse, the elected official who successfully lobbied for the Lyttelton rail tunnel) has changed very little in 50 years. Changes to its traffic are vast. In the mid-70s, bicycles and motorbikes would jostle equally for the spaces between the cars at red lights. The simple way to tell one from the other at a glance was that motorcyclists wore helmets while cyclists didn't. When the lights changed green, numerous 2-strokes zoomed away and joined as pairs in each lane, leaving trails of blue smoke, while the 10-speed bikes rushed for the relative safety of the left side of the road. It seems unimaginable today. But for a start, the gap between two modern Corollas with wing mirrors is a cycle width less than between two Morris 1300s in a day when cars went without exterior mirrors. In addition, lower vehicle roof lines aided visibility for the two wheelers. The large numbers of Japanese 2-stroke 'bikes had stemmed from the Kirk government's relaxation of hire purchase regulations. 10-speed bicycles, made in New Zealand, became the poor man's 2-stroke. Every day the same spectacle could be seen from the Tait Sales and Service Branch at 223 Moorhouse Ave.

By the mid-70s Tait Electronics had a broad base of customer types. Taxi companies and emergency services were the largest users but most organisations having large fleets such as utility companies, long haul and delivery companies, security companies and roading contractors were also big users. Smaller businesses such as real estate companies with several sales agents or an electrical contractor with several vehicles were often Tait customers. Sole traders could be customers too, either with a basestation manned by the wife at home or via a call centre, a favourite of the day being "Seekers". A potential customer would have his or her requirement assessed by a sales representative. A first consideration was always coverage area. Almost always, radio telephones worked through a repeater and it was the repeater that defined the coverage area. For example, the east of Christchurch together with Lyttelton were best covered by the Mt Pleasant repeater while the Marley's Hill repeater gave the best coverage to the west of Christchurch and out over the Canterbury Plains. Having established the most suitable repeater, channel selection was next. Large fleets generally had their own channel but smaller operators shared channels. There was no privacy, all users on any particular channel could not block out the conversations of the others. Instead, users were sensibly chosen so that competing businesses didn't share the same channel. Sometimes the lack of privacy had advantages as with the wreckers' channel. If the car wrecker you went to didn't have the part you wanted, he would pick up his mic and describe the part. Any wrecker that had that part in stock would then reply. This saved a lot of driving or telephoning. Tait sets had options for up to 6 channels so that operators who travelled the country could be allocated a repeater channel wherever they were. Because VHF (very high frequency) is line-of-sight, channels could be reused every few hundred kilometres without interfering with each other. After settling on the most suitable repeater(s) and available channel(s) a contract was drawn up. The branch or dealer would then supply and install the equipment.

To be active on any channel a radiotelephone needed a pair of crystals, one to set the receiver on channel and the other to set the transmitter on channel. These accurately set the frequency to well within a kilohertz of the channel frequency and were made to order by any of several New Zealand suppliers. In metal cans measuring about 12x10x5mm, they had two wire leads protruding from the bottom that soldered into the circuitboard. The receive crystal is visible bottom centre in the cover photograph, just below the square silver component with orange centre. Crystals were fitted by technical staff at a branch or dealer after which the run-up process was repeated one final time. Tait product of the 70s and early 80s slid into dedicated cradles and these could be installed independently of radio preparation. Vehicle installations took up to two hours. Some car models allowed for quicker installation than others. For example in the HQ Holden of the era, the underside of the dash sloped toward the footwell, making the ideal mounting position for the cradle, attached by its three self-tapping screws. Space in an existing grommet allowed for passage of the DC cables through the firewall to the battery. These were soldered directly to the battery terminals using a 250 or 300 Watt soldering iron. This technique not only economised on parts, but provided the cleanest source of DC in the vehicle. For the loudspeaker, the mounting bracket was screwed down onto the transmission tunnel through the carpet. The best position for the antenna was always centre roof because the flat metal surface acted as a "ground plane". Routing of the antenna's coaxial cable was easier than might be imagined. The secret was the "inner" from an old mechanical speedo cable. After removing the rubber moulding from above the passenger's door, the head-lining could be peeled away locally after which the speedo cable could be manipulated down through the A-pillar to the region behind the dash and then pulled back after first attaching the antenna coax to it. The second step of pulling the coax from the passenger's door region, over the head-lining and through the roof-centre hole, was accomplished in a similar way but with lacing wire. After fitting the antenna, the final step was tuning it. A back to back Red Range connector pair with antenna pins diverted to coaxial cables was used to route the antenna signal via a Bird Through-Line Power Meter. This meter could measure both forward power to the antenna and reverse power, reflected back from it. The whip antennae were simply lengths of 3mm diameter stainless steel wire and pruning them to optimum length would result in maximum forward power together with near zero reflected power.

No process will run day after day under time pressure, for months without mishap. The electric drills used at the branch were made by Desoutter. These were small, and delivered high torque at low rpm. The torque was achieved through gearing with the result that when the trigger was released, it took a few seconds for the high speed armature to come to a stop. Automotive carpets were often looped pile types. When drilling mounting holes in the vehicle floor, occasionally the drill bit would snag the carpet yarn and as this wound around the bit, a ladder would begin in the carpet. If noticed in time and with luck, the drill would wind to a stop before the ladder got beyond the mounting bracket. Before my time at the branch an unfortunate technician had apparently got a short circuit from the battery live terminal to the radio chassis, which then found an earth through the coax braid to the centre roof antenna. Prior to any awareness of what was happening, the short circuit current got the coax so hot that it singed a track in the head-lining! Fortunately the management culture was such that honest mistakes were accepted. This resulted in a two way street where employees could be up front about what went wrong thus leaving the workshop foreman in a knowledgeable position from where he could chart the best solution for the customer.

In the mid-70s, 223 Moorhouse Ave was a busy place. It had been built as a two storey house a few generations earlier. It was situated toward the front of the section and the neighbouring house to the west had been demolished leaving sufficient space for a wide driveway. At the back, on the east side was a wooden shack affectionately known as "the basher", which had been set up for the manufacture of antennae. Elsewhere there was shingle. The north boundary included a dogleg. Before my time there, the crew had pranked a colleague by manhandling his car sideways into the gap between the dogleg and basher! An open ended lean-to on the back of the house served as the service bay and was just large enough for two cars to nose in. Getting trucks under cover was out of the question but there was ample room for them in the yard. First impressions count for everything, right? Imagine you are a new customer in 1975. You've parked your car in the yard and walk to the only door you can see, the one under the lean-to. You pull the door open to be greeted by ancient brown linoleum and immediately see a coin on the floor. Just as your fingers discover that the coin is glued to the lino, the spring return door hits you in the rear! You look up to be greeted by laughter from an ever so slightly greying, modified early Beatles haircut. You had just met Norm, or at least, his lighter side. When I started there 1977, foot traffic had worn the image off the coin.

Norman Clark was the workshop foreman. Usually just Norm, but very occasionally Norman Forman. Norm knew the Tait customer well. But he knew their fleets even better. Although Tait sets were very reliable, occasionally Norm might be called out in the weekend to tend a problem that a customer thought couldn't wait until Monday. During one such callout, he discovered a potential issue with a fuse. During installation, an inline fuse was routinely fitted into the wire to battery-hot (usually positive but sometimes negative on older English cars). This was a plastic assembly where a spring held wire ends in contact with the fuse element. Onto each wire end, an eyelet was soldered. Wires were stripped slightly short so that a nice looking dome of solder would form on the end of the eyelet. Norm discovered poor contact between the solder dome on the eyelet and the solder on the end of the fuse element. He attributed this to engine fumes promoting the buildup of a film of "vertigrease" on the solder and then immediately imagined the fix. Simply strip the wires a little longer so that copper strands would protrude through the solder dome and "bight" into the fuse end. Problem solved. In a callout to a basestation problem many months later, he discovered poor contact within a BNC coaxial connector. By suggesting a change to where the braid was trimmed during connector assembly, he was able to eliminate the problem from the future.

There was no hint of management featherbedding at 223 Moorhouse Ave. The branch manager, Bruce Campbell, occupied a small room upstairs. The largest upstairs room served as the staff cafeteria. A ground floor room at front was occupied by two receptionists. They once had a frightening experience there, when a delivery truck backed into their front window, and described how they saw the frame and glass slowly deform and then fracture as the vehicle inched very slowly backwards. There was another room between the receptionists' and Norm's room with the coin. It was occupied by three experienced technicians, Des McNickel, Burt van Dissel and Des Philpott, the latter two having appeared in the "last 8" and "first 12" photographs (page viii). I appreciated the wisdom of these three "old timers", as they then appeared to me. On Monday mornings, after rolling up in his faded green Commer van, Burt usually gave an update on the weekend's progress on the batch he was building in Duvauchelle. Des McNickel had relatives in the same South Canterbury area covered by a hay carting contractor that I'd worked for during summer holidays and also talked of his passion for music. Des Philpott reminisced of a Williamson Amplifier. The design was first published in 1947 and was considered the best of the post war years. Des described how he and some friends scrimped and saved to buy the collection of parts. Knowing they could never afford the output transformer, they decided to make their own. Des told how they dismantled an old mains transformer for its core, lit a bonfire on the lawn and threw in the laminations to anneal them. They then constructed the transformer according to the Williamson transformer winding data. The story didn't end there. Next came the bass reflex loudspeaker. "Almost as big as a telephone box." Des mentioned with a smile. In those times, there were live radio broadcasts of the organ in a Wellington cathedral. Des went on to describe how they could put a candle in the bass port and see the bass notes cause the flame to flicker. Eventually they saved enough money for a genuine transformer. But Des thought it never sounded quite as good as their homemade one! This middle room had been the scene of a masterful prank a few years earlier. A technician, who had since moved on, had always kept a jumbled desk with test equipment precariously stacked. His two colleagues thought he needed a lesson. They joined two syringes with a long tube and filled the system with water. One syringe was connected to a precariously placed test instrument while the other was hidden on a perpetrator's bench so that the test instrument could be moved remotely and secretly. The way the perpetrators told the story was quite amusing. "As the victim reached up to

A Loftin White amplifier of unknown manufacture. Designed in 1929 and acknowledged as the first HiFi amplifier, it predates the Williamson by almost 20 years. At centre a 300B replaces the original 252 output triode. Temporary modifications at left allow a 5Y3 to stand in for an 81 half wave rectifier valve. At right an EF86 mounts on an adapter that replaces an unavailable tetrode valve.

adjust the instrument, we moved it. The guy suddenly reached up with both hands to save it while making a subdued gasp. So we both asked: is everything ok? Yeah, yeah... all good. So we then waited until he was in deep concentration and moved it again. A louder gasp!" And so they went on with gleeful grins.

Returning again to Norm's room, this had benches to accommodate up to 5 other people. Occupation here was fluid. Some benches had basic test equipment while others were for paperwork only. There is a long list of names due to the way trainee technicians moved around the company. In no particular order, Paul Daigneault, Paul Morrison, Paul Johnston, Brian Peck, Rob Morrison, Gary ??? and, before my time there, Alastair Lang and Steve Kozanic. Steve was determined that he would one day own a Mazda RX-7, impossible on a New Zealand technician's wage. He went to Australia and when I met him there in 1984, he owned an RX-7! A tech whose name escapes me drove a beautifully restored Model A. Discrete engine modifications gave it a cruising speed of 70mph. Once during the festive season he took a Model A load of us to the Dux where we enjoyed lunch. On the way back down the one-way toward the Bridge of Remembrance, he set the hand throttle, opened the door and hopped out to drive from the running board, one hand steering and the other yahooing.

In the old house there were not the number of wall outlets that an electronic workshop should have had. One lone wall outlet supported 6 or 7 tapon plugs, the stack always on the verge of sagging under its weight. Occasionally many test instruments on many benches would go dark when a circuit breaker tripped. There would always be a rush to the switchboard to cool the offending breaker with CRC Freeze before clacking it back on. Opposite the coin was the door to the washroom with toilet having its own door within. The toilet held evidence of a prank from earlier years in the form of a circular scorch mark on the floor. Someone had in their possession a metre or so of the kind of yellow fuse used for explosives. This type of fuse usually held a curve after being cut from the spool it came on. So the one metre loop of fuse, without detonator of course, was lit both ends and slid under the toilet door to the consternation of the unfortunate occupant... There were three or four other rooms in the old house that were occupied by sales personnel.

The names of most of the sales people escape me, but not some of the jokes. For example: "The sign outside the Synagogue: We Keep the Piece"! A later joke from Field Engineering followed on from this. "One rabbi kept the pieces and sewed them into a purse. He found it useful as

A matching 3-pin plug and cord socket designed and produced by a Christchurch supplier of electrical products. Norm told how his wife worked at that same company at the same time as he worked at Tricity House. So esteemed was Tricity House and its staff that Norm's Wife would occasionally be asked to bring things home for Norm's appraisal. The idea was that the teardrop shape would make for easy nighttime connection. So Norm described how he turned the lights out and began gently stabbing in the dark. The pair he was given were shaped identically. To his horror one of the stabs resulted in an offset engagement, a highly dangerous situation. When this was reported back, the side bulges were added. The photograph illustrates how these prevent the offset engagement.

luggage because when he rubbed it, it turned into a suitcase." The sales people were gentlemen and totally unlike the pushy salesmen of the shady car yard. They all had good knowledge of repeater coverage together with excellent Tait product knowledge and could always understand the customers' needs. There were often sales to rural customers which required basestation equipment to be installed as away jobs. One of the sales staff, whose name I think I remember, sometimes came along driving his grey HQ Holden, not to keep tabs but to keep in touch with his customer. He had previously been a traveller for a record company and upon learning I enjoyed classical music, gave me some leftover sample records including Sibelius' symphony number three and Dvorak's Piano Quintet and American String Quartet. After moving along from the branch I learnt that Giff had lost his life to an acute medical event just short of age 40. RIP Gifford. Most of the away jobs went well but one exception is possibly worth a mention. On the main street in Rangiora there was a two storey building having quite a steep hip roof. From memory, the ground floor had hosted a paint shop while the first floor was occupied by some commercial tenants. The job was to install a sleeve dipole, a type of omnidirectional antenna, on the ridge. The rear of the building had a first floor exterior walkway accessible via an outside staircase. I carried the ladder up these stairs and placed it on the walkway with its feet against the base of the balustrade such that it couldn't slide out. After a first ascent to assess things like mounting base position and guy wire anchor points, I went back to the van for all the necessary tools and equipment. When I returned, I found the ladder lying neatly on the walkway and assumed that one of the tenants must have placed it there. After putting it back and ascending again, the job was half way through when the sound of a gentle swish followed by a loud thud exposed my bad assumption about the ladder. It hadn't been placed on the walkway, it had blown down. This second time, it left me stranded. Everything needed to finish the job was to hand so it made sense to continue working in the hope that a tenant would appear and offer to put the ladder back. No such luck. After finishing and then moving tools and leftovers to where the ladder should have been, it was time to take the situation seriously. Tenants didn't immediately respond to calls for assistance. When someone did finally appear, it was not with the look of sympathy expected. It was with the look of contemptuous anger. "Why did you leave that ladder to endanger my staff?" he demanded. What did he think this was? The 2020s where even flat roofs have ladder support brackets and harness anchor wires? No, this was the mid-70s. But there was no choice other than to savour the taste of humble pie and graciously accept the derision. There was just no other way down.

One interesting installation was the Taxi Alarm. Assaults on taxi drivers were not unheard of. Tait responded by designing a silent alarm system. There were examples of assailants yanking the microphone cord from the radiotelephone and trying to snap the antenna. The latter was not a problem, because even from a broken antenna, enough signal will escape. The critical components were a hidden microphone and a hidden activation switch, usually foot operated. When activated, a series of warning beeps would be transmitted, the hidden mic would go live and the radiotelephone's controls would be bypassed. The driver would then converse with the hijacker and try to discretely drop his or her location into the conversation. The taxi headquarters would then advise the police of the location. The system resulted in apprehensions, often witnessed by the many other taxies that had gone to help.

All jobs were well recorded. Each tech had a carbon copy manifold book. Norm was a stickler for accuracy here and could always explain why to any doubters. He would explain that the managers of the big fleets could have difficulty in keeping tabs on all their vehicles and drivers and that if every invoice had date of work, vehicle type and number plate, radio type and serial number, everything stayed simple. To the contrary, filling in the blanks later would consume much time at both the Tait end and the customer end. This was reminiscent of a story I was told as a child. A farmer had bought a new saddle from his stock and station agent. At the time of purchase, the experienced staff were occupied and so a relatively new lad assisted the farmer. The lad had not wished to appear rude by enquiring of the farmer's name but none of the experienced staff had seen and identified the farmer either. Through a process of elimination, management were able to narrow it down to five possible farmers. From there it would be a simple matter to bill all five and wait to see who paid... But all five paid! The manager, Bruce Campbell, had seen the limitations of the Moorhouse Ave site and took it upon himself to improve the situation. He moved the operation to a purpose designed building at 210 Main South Road, Sockburn. The word was that the whole project had been his baby. He had found the land, had the building designed to his requirements, got quotes and organised the mortgage. It was luxury compared to Moorhouse Ave. There was room for three trucks under cover. Doors at each end allowed trucks to enter from a back street and then depart out onto the main road. After I had left there and gone to field engineering, I heard a couple of interesting anecdotes. One of the salesmen had been in the cafeteria when technicians were complaining about poor wages. When he suggested that they were doing ok, they said to him, "You might come to work one morning and find we've all resigned in protest." The salesman replied, "That's ok, I'd just go outside and shake the tree and a few more will fall down!" After that he said he wasn't too popular for a while. At another time a Ministry of Transport traffic patrol motorbike was in for some radiotelephone work. When finished, the technician took it out for a test drive. On the way back into the building, he tried to startle his colleagues with a blast from the mechanical siren. Got a serious telling off from the management he said! Apparently there was no coin glued to the floor in this new building.

Radiotelephone Person

On the north west side of the circular saw building at 558 Wairakei Rd, was a grassed area with trees and wooden picnic tables. This was the site of a mid-80s photograph of the engineering staff (page viii). In the absence of a boundary fence along Wairakei Rd, the picnic tables were chained to the trees. This prompted a newsletter to suggest that the Tait Conservation effort was very successful, noting that since the chains were fitted, no trees had been stolen! It was here that many in engineering gathered to watch an overflight of a Warbirds Spitfire in the late 80s. As well as being popular for lunch, it was often the site of an annual staff picnic. At such gatherings, Angus would always do his best to get around as many people as he could. It was at one such gathering where he said to me, "I've got a lot of very good engineers, but not many radiotelephone people." Understanding what this statement means, requires a trip back in time.

From the late 40s through and into the 60s, Angus had single handedly designed complete radiotelephones. Totally absurd today, but 60 plus years ago, not quite so. The impressive achievement was made possible, in part, by the radio shop. In the 1960s, my father was the manager of a farm in West Otago. He was an avid reader of nonfiction including military history, especially if cavalry were involved, and frequent visitor to the secondhand bookshop, even once finding a 6th edition of Darwin's Origin of Species. A good shepherd, he claimed to be non-technical but had good general knowledge and a good understanding of farm machinery. The owner in residence of the farm was mechanically and technically adept, as in fact were many farmers. My father explained to me many years later that he sometimes found that a frustration. "Early start tomorrow, we'll plough such and such a paddock." the boss had said. So my father started early only to find the boss had started earlier still and pulled the plough to bits. I remember repairs to that old plough. It had needed a felt washer and one was ordered from the local garage, about 70 mm diameter with 35 mm hole, but when it arrived the boss thought it too thick and soft and so made one himself, the material being cut from the brim of his felt hat. He had never been without his grey felt hat and still wasn't, continuing to wear it with a hole in the brim above one ear. This eccentric farm owner had been a radio hobbyist in his youth. He described how radio stations in America could be received on almost any night and that details of the broadcast, including callsign, time, frequency and programme, would be written down and mailed to the station. In the weeks that followed, the station would send their QSL card by return mail. During the war he had been posted to the Pacific as a radar operator. As kids, my brothers and I were very disappointed by his answer when we asked him about the enemy he detected, "Two whales and a friendly submarine." The war was far from forgotten in the early 60s, our mother sometimes speaking of her own experiences after enlisting with the ATS or Auxiliary Territorial Service in the UK where she had operated the optical range finder at a coastal AA gun battery. Although the German bombing campaigns were over by the time she joined, she did experience a "tip and run" raid by a lone FW-190. Due to outdated intelligence, only an old unused command post was bombed but a following strafing run did claim one casualty. Also in the Kelso community but in a different WWII posting, the headmaster of the Primary School had been a radar technician. I remember him telling the class how, during a cold night and in the absence of a heater, they had made their own by wrapping some resistance wire around a brick. Other than that he said nothing of the war. Twenty years on, it must have been difficult to know just how much of radar was still classified. The farm owner did praise the ability of the technicians and how they could diagnose a problem from how the symptoms developed "...and sometimes you weren't paying as much attention as you should have been." he added. Twenty years on from WWII

Opposite Page:

Drake's 1933
Jones 1937
RSGB 1965
ARRL 1969

JONES RADIO HANDBOOK 1937 EDITION
THE
AMATEUR
RADIO
HANDBOOK
RSGB
R.S.G.B.
FORTY-SIXTH EDITION
1969

radar, electronic appliances were still unreliable. In radios, older but common rectifier valves (80 and 5Y3) often had filaments go open circuit. Valves performing the other functions were "indirectly heated" and rarely failed unless pushed to the limit as was often the case in television sets. Electrolytic capacitors were very unreliable, often failing after a few short years. Paper/foil capacitors often suffered from moisture ingress and carbon composition resistors could be unreliable if they ran a little hot. Only one thing made radio possible; the radio shop.

The town of Kelso was too small to have a radio shop. Tapanui, a dozen kilometres away, had two, Hewson's being my go-to. For a crystal set, I bought the coil and diode from a Dunedin shop and the variable capacitor from Hewson's. A long aerial wire from an Oregon or redwood tree to a brick chimney was the final ingredient. On a subsequent visit to Hewson's I asked: What's next? The technician lifted the ball point pen from behind his ear and drew the schematic for a one valve radio. It is this aspect of the radio shop that is relevant to A M Tait Ltd, with Angus himself having cut his teeth in an Oamaru radio shop after leaving Waitaki Boys High School at age 17 as a radio hobbyist. More often than not, radio shop staff were home constructors. Many were ham radio operators and built their own transmitting and receiving equipment. Many built various items of test equipment. In the 60s, some even built their own television sets. Some of the craft was taught, some passed from peer to peer and a great deal was often self-taught with the help of good books and periodicals. One of the most famous began as *Marconigraph* in 1911 before changing its name to *Wireless World* in 1913. Austin C Lescarboura, managing editor of Scientific American, released his book, *Radio for Everybody* in England in 1922. In 1926 the American Radio Relay League, ARRL, released the first edition of *The Radio Amateur's Handbook*. *Drake's Radio Cyclopedia* was first published in 1927. Some entries were trivial, others not. Difficult entries made reference to other entries which could be easily looked up in turn due to the alphabetical order. This was not unlike today's procedure of following links in a web site. There were various radio engineering

A 1940s vintage One Valve Radio recovered from a shed in Springston but of similar design to the later Tapanui radio shop drawing. A modern repair includes a valve socket adapter. Originally published in a 1936 Popular Mechanics, the design was taken up by the Australian Lamphouse magazine and given the name Hiker's One. Headphones connect at front. Aerial and earth connections through plywood, at left.

handbooks, a famous one being due to Frank C Jones and published in 1937. Its cover lists the price as "One Dollar Fifty Cents". In Britain, the first edition of *The Amateur Radio Handbook* was released by the Radio Society of Great Britain, RSGB, in 1938. *Practical Wireless* magazine began in 1932. Whereas Wireless World had been aimed more at the professional, Practical Wireless was aimed more at the hobbyist. A sister magazine, *Practical Television* began in 1934.

In Britain, 405-line black and white TV broadcasting began in 1936. During a visit to the Vintage Radio Museum, Dulwich, London in the mid-90s, I watched TV on sets manufactured before the war. The signal came from a 625 to 405 line converter. This was a double 19-inch rack of equipment occupying the last available space in the semidetached house, being an area of floor beside the live-in curator's bed. The entire dwelling had been consumed by an immense vintage radio and TV collection. Without the war, television would have advanced differently. But without TV, the war may have advanced disastrously. There were many similarities between early television and early radar, among which, they both used the cathode ray tube for the display and both operated in the VHF (very high frequency) bands. The 1933 edition of Drake's Radio Cyclopedia contains no mention of VHF or UHF (ultra high frequency). Frank C Jones' 1937 Radio Handbook includes a chapter on UHF, which includes the frequencies now denoted VHF. The chapter contains some transmitter and receiver designs, the latter being very basic and totally unsuited for use in television. In the late 1930s it was British television and radar that represented the avant guard of VHF receiver design. Angus went off to war as a radiotelephone person and after his time involved with airborne radar, returned to New Zealand as a VHF radiotelephone person.

Airborne Radar information:
https://www.dos4ever.com/EF50/EF50.html
The EF50, the Tube that helped Win the War. Ronald Dekker

The Hybrid Sets

The sets immediately preceding the T152 were built with semiconductor technology replacing valves wherever possible. These were known as the hybrid sets and were produced throughout the 60s. The Tait sets before then were fully based on the earlier technology, going by the name Valve or Vacuum Tube in the English speaking world. The former name is from the UK and goes back to Fleming's Oscillation Valve of 1904. De Forest invented the triode in the USA in 1906 and initially called it the "Audion". The eventual American name, tube, stemmed from the evacuated glass tubes that the devices were made in. Here, the term "valve" will be used because it was the accepted term in the New Zealand of the day and also, for the America term to be authentic it would need to be pronounced "toob". As an aside, glass tube is designated by its diameter expressed in units of eighths of an inch. For example the post war 9-pin valves extensively used in the Tait hybrid sets were made from glass tube of nominal size T 6½ = 13/16 inch nominal diameter, up to 7/8 inch maximum. The same nomenclature was shared with light bulbs. For example the small 12v MR16 spot lamp gets its name from having an outer diameter of 16 eighths, or two inches.

One of the oldest Tait photographs features a debonair Angus Tait standing beside a car whose open boot hosts an early Tait radiotelephone, probably a T4. The T initially stood for "type". Product "types" included many ancillary products and were numbered sequentially, with some structure beginning to appear either side of 1970. The T4 is from before the era of transistors, from a time when valves held all the glory. The valve gave worldwide radio communication, broadcast radio, talking movies, television, radar, navigation systems that allowed both sides to devastate their opponent's cities by night during WWII and the first computers.

History paints a harsh picture of valve reliability. The ENIAC Computer had needed one valve replacement every day or two. But this computer contained almost 18,000 valves. It follows that something with just 18 valves would need valve replacement only every thousand days or two. Unless valves were pushed to their limits, as they often were in television sets, they were reliable enough. As transistors became mainstream, valve reliability was not the main driver of change. The main drivers were miniaturisation, cost and power consumption, the latter being important for

A mock-up of the early Tait picture, on display at the Tait Museum.

radiotelephones that were powered from a motor vehicle's electrical system. Early transistors were slow to develop but every year or two, yet another function once performed exclusively by the valve, fell within the domain of the transistor. The hybrid sets developed in step, with valves being replaced by transistors wherever possible. The last of the hybrids, the Century Series T101, was all transistorised except for one valve. Just the heater, or filament, of this valve drew a steady 0.45 Ampere. The total

The title block and picture tube of the T90 Tait television schematic. Information at the Tait Museum makes reference to a mid-1960s tie up between A M Tait Ltd and Dreco, Dominion Radio and Electrical Corporation.

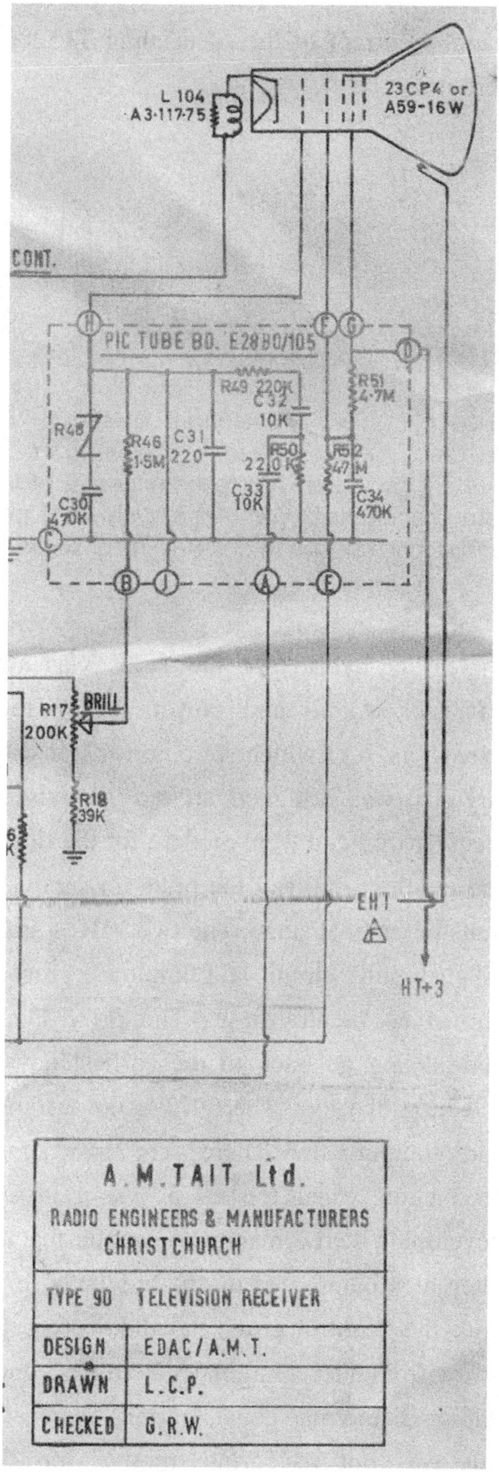

standby current of the succeeding T152 was just a quarter of this heater current.

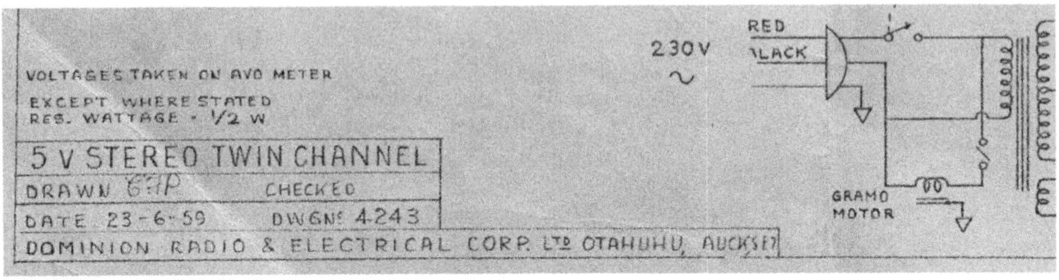

Title block and transformer of the 5 V Stereo, Dominion Radio and Electrical Corp or Dreco. 5 V refers to the 5 valve lineup. One in the power supply, two in an AM receiver typical of the day and one in each 3 Watt amplifier channel. With the efficient loudspeakers of the time, 3 Watts were more than enough to entertain neighbours.

An earlier hybrid set, the T82F, was almost equal measure valve and transistor. Audio and power supply functions were performed by 9 transistors, 6 of which were power transistors. All transmitter and receiver circuitry was designed around 10 valves. The two valves used in the receiver frontend were modern for the time, being first released in 1960 for use in television. But the prize for innovation must go to one facet of the transmitter final stage. The two valves are configured in what is known as a "push-pull" circuit and employ a cross-coupled version of a technique known as "neutralising". The prize is not for these as push-pull and neutralising go back to the earliest days of radio. The prize is for the selection of valve. The 6973 is not a transmitting valve but rather, a hi-fi audio output valve. There were already many good audio output valves in production when the 6973 was released in 1957 and aimed at the developing stereo market. A unique feature of the 6973 was the way the internal structure was married to the base. Pairs of direct connections from both the "control grid" and the "screen grid" efficiently conducted heat away from these internal electrodes, out the pins and into the socket. Although thermal considerations were always important in transmitters, this was not the prime motive for choosing the 6973. Almost by

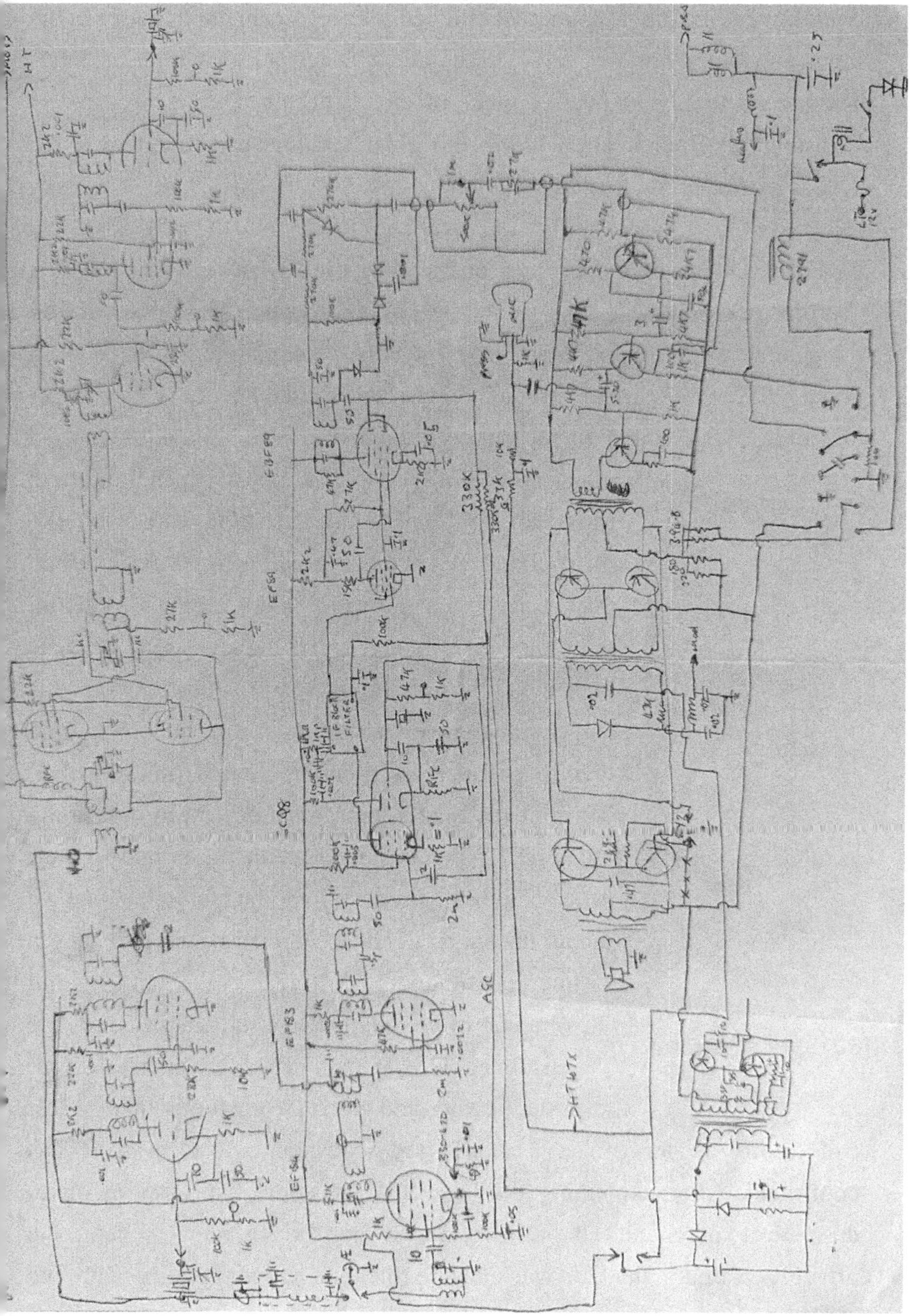

My hand drawn T82F schematic, copied from an old original in the absence of a photocopier at the Moorhouse Ave branch.

coincidence, the pin arrangement allowed for perfect shielding between the input and output of the valve, essential at frequencies as high as VHF. This was a highly innovative piece of circuit design. During my time at Christchurch Branch in 1977/78, the older technicians remembered the T82 as a good product and good money maker.

Radiotelephones of these times and earlier used what was known as a "carbon microphone". This same type of microphone was also used in telephones of the same era. Their internal construction consisted of a powder of fine carbon granules between a diaphragm and another electrode. When sound waves caused the diaphragm to vibrate, the carbon granules behind it were compressed and rarefied, thus varying the electrical resistance of the microphone in sympathy with the voice. When powered by a suitable DC current, carbon microphones provided much higher output voltages than their dynamic counterparts. Unfortunately this audio signal level tended to deteriorate over time due to the carbon granules coagulating together. Norm at the branch took great delight in describing the issue, "When customers came in saying that their office couldn't hear them over the radiotelephone we did an instant fix." The technician would pick up the microphone and bash it against the nearest solid object, often to the visual dismay of the customer. This "repair" shook the granules back into a powder and when the customer made a test call to his or her office, a much improved sound level was always confirmed. After explaining this standard procedure, Norm went on to describe a more unusual problem. A van had driven into the yard, the driver explaining that he was new to the job and unfamiliar with the radiotelephone. He said that the office had given him a quick demonstration on their base unit but then when he was driving, couldn't

T82 Carbon Microphone

work out how to reply to their calls. Norm told how he went to the van to find that the microphone was not on its usual hook. "It was a forward control vehicle with the engine cover between the front seats," Norm went on, "...the van had obviously been in for service, and the mechanic hadn't noticed that the mic had fallen into the engine bay when he closed the cover." Norm then explained that when he opened the engine cover and pulled the cord out, the microphone had gone. It had rubbed off onto the road! By the time of the Century Series, the carbon mic had been superseded by the better sounding dynamic mic because its lower voltage output was easily amplified by the transistorised modulator circuit.

I encountered the Tait T101 of the Century Series at the Tait service branch when it occupied the old weatherboard two storey house at 223 Moorhouse Avenue. The T101 had been a contemporary of the Pye Cambridge. Both of these products were heavy and large, being about the size of the smallest PC tower case. Although only the transmitter sections used valves, the transistor circuits that provided modulation and high voltage generation functions had heavy transformers and bulky heatsinks. Norm, the Tait service foreman had worked some of his life as a repair technician at Tricity House, 209a Manchester Street, one of New Zealand's highly respected radio shops. His view was that the Pye Cambridge was a better product than the T101. As a technician trainee, most of my time at the service branch was spent installing Tait radiotelephones in cars, with just a little time on the bench doing service work. From an overall perspective I remember the T101 as being well engineered. For example much of the receiver was in a removable module. Sheet metal protrusions each end slid between guides in the chassis to give accurate connector engagement when it was refitted. The detent mechanism which held it in place deserves mention. Ball bearings in the guides engaged holes in the sheet metal protrusions. Spire nuts provided spring tension, the ball being held under the "thread". IE, the ball located the Spire nut and Spire nut provided the spring tension. It was a very simple yet effective mechanism.

When I had encountered the Century Series sets in 1977, they were almost 10 years old. John Croft, one of the "last eight" (page viii) and "first twelve", had had no input into their initial design but when I worked under him in the early 80s, he told me some of his experience with them. He described one circuit, in the IF (intermediate frequency) from memory, that had had a propensity to oscillate and found that its design had unwittingly included a "textbook oscillator". John mentioned that each Century Series product sold had to be brought in for warranty service about 10 times. He gave the example of crystal sockets. The spring contacts in these were so poor that John had wondered if their manufactures had used annealed copper by mistake. These setbacks must have contributed to the failing of the A M Tait company.

John's reminiscence of the crystal socket issue had been prompted by the supply of some substandard components during the early 1980s. At this time there were three senior engineers; one for mobile radios, one for basestation equipment and John for the handheld product. The first Tait handheld, into which John had had considerable design input, was the UHF T303. This had a 12 Volt battery pack that attached to the bottom of the radio. The pack contained 12, 0.5Ah, AA sized nickel cadmium cells. The battery pack could be dropped into a dedicated charger with or without the radio attached. One highlight of the battery and charger combination was the one-hour fast charge capability. This feature called for sophisticated end-of-charge detection and so in addition to a voltage cutoff in the charger, there was a temperature cutoff function in the battery pack. The original temperature cutoff devices were reliable, but a later alternative part was not. These had continued to be purchased and used after the first hints of trouble. John saw the parallel with the Century Series crystal socket debacle and offered a mirth laced solution. Components were normally booked out of the store against an order number, with each production run having its unique number. Components requested by service or by engineering had a fixed number, but components would be released to these numbers only if they were not required for production.

John mockingly suggested the need for an order number which would take priority above all else so that dud components could be requested and immediately directed under a big hammer so that they could not thereafter damage the company brand! All joking aside, the T101 crystal sockets had contributed to the failure of AM Tait Ltd. However, good customer support goes a long way toward negotiating teething troubles in new products. When Angus Tait "put the boat out again" with Tait electronics, he had the full respect of staff, suppliers, bankers and customers alike.

The All Transistor T152

While Angus was working to establish A M Tait Ltd in the late 1940s, the transistor was being invented in the USA. The name stems from trans~~fer~~ ~~re~~sistor. First came the point-contact transistor, invented by William Shockley's colleagues, John Bardeen and Walter Brattain in December 1947. The next month, Shockley himself invented the junction transistor. All worked for Bell Laboratories and all shared the Nobel Prize in Physics in 1956. There was a long gestation to commercial reality, beginning with licenses to the technology being offered for twenty five thousand dollars. Texas Instrument were early to partake and released the world's first transistor radio in Q4 1954 under the brand name Regency. Named the TR-1, it was small enough to fit in a business shirt pocket of the era. Lagging by a whole year, Sony responded with a larger product, their TR-55, and stole the market as the rest of the world looked on helplessly. The capability of transistors developed progressively and they were introduced into Tait designs accordingly. Tait sets using both valves and transistors were referred to as hybrid sets. For example, in the T82F, germanium power transistors replaced expensive vibrating reeds in power supplies. They also replaced valves in the modulator and loudspeaker amplifier circuits. In the last of the hybrid sets, the Century Series, all circuitry was transistorised with the exception of the transmitter power stages.

The smartphone I'm writing this on contains about 16 billion transistors, making it all too easy to assume that transistors were always easy to use. Presumably it was my father who found "How to Build an Inexpensive TRANSISTOR RADIO" "a Beta Book for Boys", during one of his frequent bookshop visits. The one-transistor design called for an OC44 transistor. The good news was that it was available from Hewson's radio shop in Tapanui. The bad news was the price, 14s 6d meaning fourteen shillings and sixpence. Some "choconomics" can put this in perspective. In the mid-1960s, this amount of money bought 29 Crunchy Bars at 6d each. Today, 29 crunchy bars cost about $60. As an eleven year old, 14s 6d amounted to 3/4 of my life's savings. But it turned out to be money well spent because the radio worked. The instructions highlighted just one of the fallibilities of transistors. They were prone to damage by heat. It was recommended when soldering each of the 30mm long leads, that it should be gripped with pliers 10 to 20mm from the transistor itself, so as to divert the soldering heat. I don't remember having to buy any more high price transistors, for a while at least. Many in the local farming community took holidays in the Pacific islands and returned with duty-free transistor radios. Perhaps the radio shops preferred to avoid the new technology. Customers were often told that their "tranny" was unrepairable, when the fault was as simple as broken wires at the battery holder. Any given to me that were

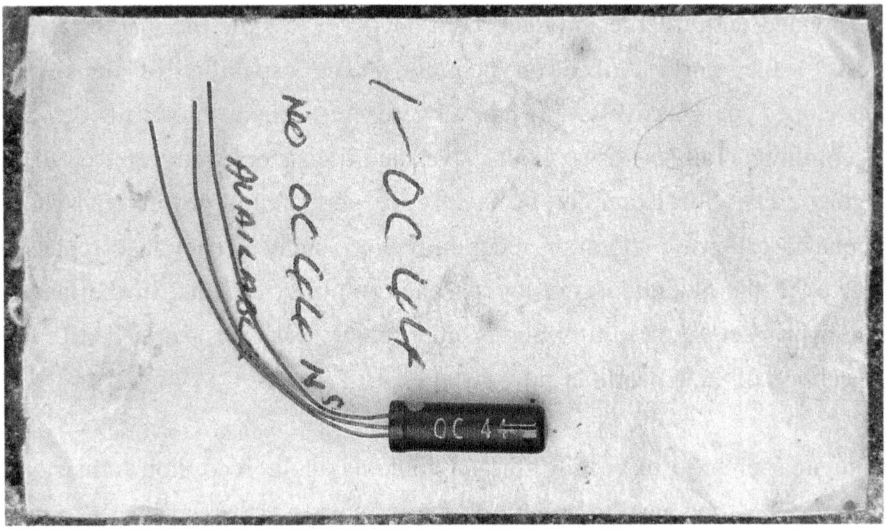

Unused OC44 with original manila packet acquired at a garage clear out circa 1990. This germanium technology was light sensitive and black paint blocked light from the transparent case. Tarnished leads, white text, red dot marks collector lead.

genuinely unrepairable became sources of parts. Any I could fix, I would offer back but some generous owners would let me keep them anyway.

Designing with valves had one major plus. Short of an accident which broke the glass, they were indestructible. This made them highly suitable for experimentation and even pushing them to the point where internal electrodes glowed red hot would not usually cause permanent damage. The red heat was no more than the message to back off soon. To the contrary, the early transistors were highly fragile. Too much voltage, too much current or too much heat during experimentation would result in immediate failure without warning. This was not the only difficulty in designing with transistors. There had been an industry agreement within New Zealand that when colour television was introduced in the early 70s, it would be fully transistorised. Yet the electronics course at the Christchurch Polytechnic in 1976 still taught at least as much valve theory as transistor theory. Perhaps this was because valve theory was established as well as straightforward. Transistor theory on the other hand is another step harder because the output affects the input, resulting in a complexity that may have been beyond mid-70s polytechnic academic levels. Fortunately, for designers wishing to introduce transistors into their products, the semiconductor manufacturers had always included application circuits in their product data. In addition to this, the periodicals and handbooks were including articles and chapters on transistors, just as they had done for valves decades earlier. Transistor circuits, if designed to work safely within the manufacturer's ratings for voltage, current, power and temperature, including during soldering, turned out to be very reliable. Valves suffered from wear-out, whereas transistors didn't. Transistors had only three, or rarely four, soldered connections. Valves had 9 pins plugging into a valve socket in addition to the 9 soldered connections of the socket. If germanium transistors didn't end the reign valves, they did put the writing on this wall. Texas Instrument invented the silicon transistor in the mid-50s. Just as for the germanium transistor before it, the silicon transistor advanced slowly but deliberately. It was far more tolerant of high

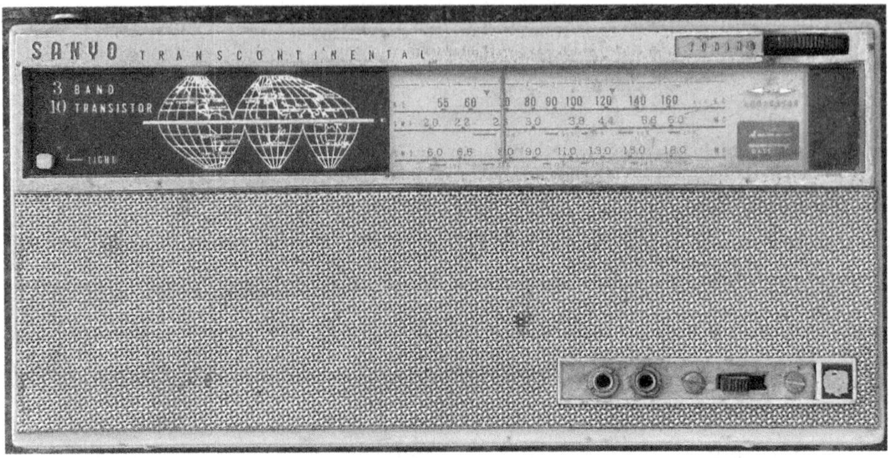

A Sanyo 10S-P10N, 1962-1968, 230 x 115 mm. Opposite: internal view

temperatures than its predecessor and lent itself well to mass production. By the late 1960s, silicon planar transistors were everywhere, as they remain today. For example, the Philips BC107 was first introduced in 1965. The original looked like a small metal can having three leads protruding from the bottom. Since then, cheaper to produce, plastic versions have become the norm and are commonplace today, with a popular surface mounted version being designated BC847. The "choconomics" derived $60 for an OC44 in the mid-1960s can buy one thousand BC847 today.

The T152 was a masterstroke of design in so many ways and set the standard for Tait product for a quarter century. It fully exploited all possible benefits offered by silicon transistors, leveraging the advantages toward smaller size, lower weight, and excellent performance when compared to anything else in New Zealand, or the world for that matter. It used the first plastic version of the BC107, the BC147 together with its opposite polarity counterpart, the BC157. These were used for audio frequencies. For radio frequencies, the BF194, also silicon, was used. In the trade, these low power transistors are known as small-signal transistors. For the loudspeaker amplifier and modulator circuits, silicon

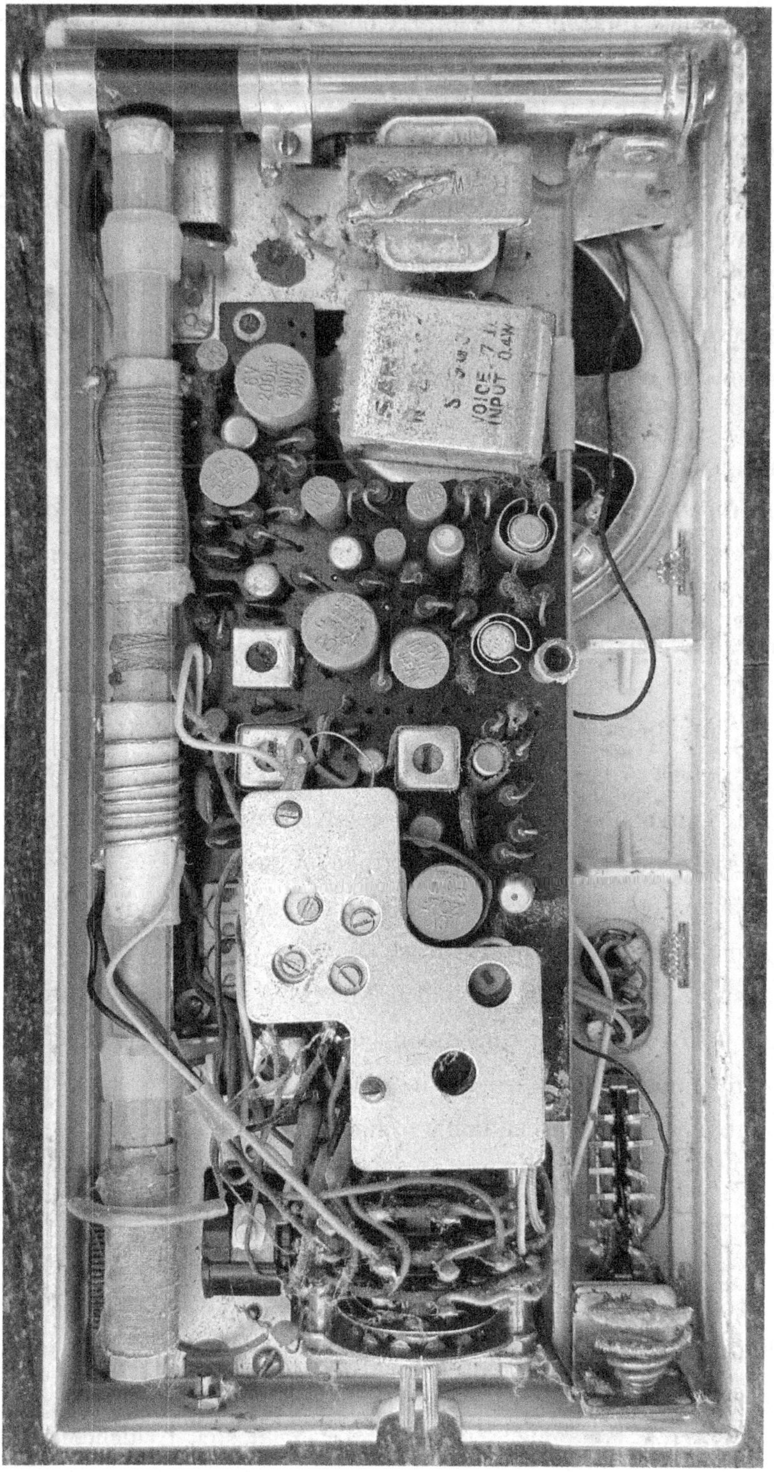

power transistors were called for. Considerable size and weight saving was to be had from these circuits. To begin with, because there were no valves, the entire 250 Volt power supply of the Century Series was no longer needed. Next, the loudspeaker amplifier design chosen obviated the need for a speaker transformer. Finally, compared to the Century Series product, everything about the T152 modulator was smaller and lighter. Four power transistors were needed in total. The BD124 chosen was very new, not appearing in overseas consumer products until 1968. But the receiver and transmitter required some special transistors not even readily available in 1968. Let's begin with the receiver. Since the 1930s nearly all receivers, including those used in WWII airborne radar, employed the superheterodyne principal as patented by Edwin Armstrong in 1920. The superheterodyne centres around a constant *intermediate frequency* or IF and allows the tuning or channel selection function to be confined to just the small part of the receiver that follows the antenna, known as the *frontend.* For VHF receivers the international standard for the IF is 10.7MHz. In the T82F and T101 the difficulty of amplifying this frequency with valves or germanium transistors forced the use of what is known as "dual conversion", where a consecutive superheterodyne converted the 10.7MHz down to 455kHz, a frequency that valves and germanium transistors could easily amplify. (Incidentally, 455kHz is the international standard IF for use in broadcast receivers.) Because the BF194 silicon transistor could easily amply 10.7MHz, the T152 was able to avoid the complexity of dual conversion. Compared to all predecessors, this improvement in the IF part of the superheterodyne was significant, but the improvements unleashed in the frontend were vast.

As previously mentioned, a modern smartphone contains about 16 billion transistors, or more specifically, 16 billion MOSFETs. (Metal Oxide of Silicon Field Effect Transistors) Mosfets were invented in 1960 and although they are the mainstay of computing chips, they have always been available individually as discrete components. A variation, also available as a discrete component, is the dual-gate mosfet. Evidence of how new these were in the late 60s can be found in the 1969 ARRL Radio Amateur's Handbook. Just three VHF dual gate mosfets are listed in the data appendix but none appear in receiver circuits in the chapter on VHF. In the T152, two of these brand new devices were designed into the frontend, the section of the receiver which follows the antenna. The first was used for the RF amplifier, the *radio frequency amplifier* being the amplifier following the antenna. The second mosfet formed the mixer, that is, the frequency changer stage that converts the wanted signal frequency to the intermediate frequency. The performance of the T152 receiver was nothing short of breathtaking. Its ability to receive very distant signals was exceptional but at the same time it rejected unwanted signals extremely well too. And yet, if the T152 receiver was breathtaking, the transmitter was in another league. Small-signal silicon transistors were inherently better at high frequencies than their germanium counterparts. But the first silicon power transistors operated at low frequencies only. It took determined efforts by the semiconductor manufacturers to push VHF transistors to successively higher powers. In the last of the hybrid sets, demands on the final transmitting transistor amounted to about half a Watt, being the drive power required by the valve transmitter stage(s). By the late 60s, VHF power transistors capable of producing 10 Watts were arriving. One of these was the last piece of the T152 puzzle. But it wasn't going to be as simple as swapping a transmitting valve for a transmitting transistor.

It was always well known at Taits, that the Tait T152, the first all transistor radiotelephone to be made in New Zealand, had been designed by John Croft. I once made the comment to John about the PAs (power amplifiers) as fitted on the backs of the T196 and T198, the Tait FM products that were developed in the late 70s. I said I marvelled at the high tech approach that involved low inductance mica capacitors (Unelco) and other advancements when compared to the current AM products such as the T162, the successor to the T152. John's reply surprised me. He said that such was the traditional approach used overseas and that he deviated from

Opposite: The failing binding of my 1971 Philips pocketbook simplified the photo taking. Note the absence of the BLY35. The stud mounted transistors shown are all of the later generation having the horizontal gold plated copper foil leads. This became the industry standard mounting method and was used for everything at Tait, including the later T152. The BLY35 is not listed in the 1969 Philips Pocketbook either, suggesting that this VHF transmitting transistor as tamed by John Croft was considered quite experimental by Philips themselves.

it when he designed the T152 with leaded components, entirely on one, single sided printed circuit board. In other words, John chose to make his own job harder so that component sourcing, circuitboard supply and assembly could all follow the established norms in New Zealand at that time. As if the job wasn't already hard enough.

Every technician in every radio shop knew of instability. Any circuit, rather than serving its intended function, such as amplifying or frequency changing, could "take off" and become its own undesirable oscillator. There could be dozens of causes. In existing designs, the condition could usually be cured by finding and replacing a faulty component. But designing with early VHF transmitting transistors was like running a gauntlet through an infinite maze of instabilities. Transmitter instability is never allowed under any circumstances as it results in unwanted interference on other users' channels. The meaning of "any circumstance" includes a broken or mismatched antenna. Special test apparatus that replicated the behaviour of the broken antenna but didn't leak radio waves into space were built for this purpose. Edison's words to the effect that invention is 1% inspiration and 99% perspiration are true to form here. Even 20 years later, designing transistorised VHF transmitters was a challenge. John's success in the late 60s was a major achievement. But there was even more to the T152 than transistors.

In 1960s New Zealand, there was a mix of positive earth and negative earth vehicles. Car radios often had a selector switch which configured the

BLY17	f_T = 70 MHz	1.5	10	I_{CBO} < 10 mA	0	40	I_{CM} = 10 A	length < 28.2
n-p-n	P_o = 40 W	1.8	40	I_{CBO} < 20 mA	0	100	V_{CER} = 100 V	width < 28.2
transmitter	G_p = 7.5 dB	1.8	40	h_{FE} = 13	−5	0	P_{tot} = 100 W	height < 10.5
h.f.	η = 55%	1.8	40	h_{FE} = 9	−10	0	T_j = 175°C	leads = 17
				C_c < 150 pF	0	40	$R_{th\,j-mb}$ = 1.5°C/mW	collector: M5
BLY37	V_{BE} < 1.5 V	0.5	5	C_c = 8 pF	0	28	I_{CM} = 2.5 A	diameter < 10
n-p-n	h_{FE} = 35	0.5	5				V_{CEO} = 36 V	height < 5.8
transmitter	f_T = 800 MHz	0.5	5				P_{tot} = 10 W	leads > 21.7
f.m.	P_i < 1.5 W	—	28				T_j = 200°C	stud length < 12
	P_o = 6 W	—	28				$R_{th\,j-h}$ = 12.5°C/W	stud: 8–32 UNC
	G_p > 6 dB	—	28					
	η > 60%	—	28					
BLY38	V_{BE} < 1.5	0.25	5	C_c = 5.5 pF	0	13.8	I_{CM} = 1.5 A	diameter < 10
n-p-n	h_{FE} = 70	0.25	5				V_{CEO} = 18 V	height < 5.8
transmitter	f_T = 1 GHz	0.25	5				P_{tot} = 5.5 W	leads > 21.7
f.m.	P_i < 0.5 W	—	13.8				T_j = 200°C	stud length < 12
	P_o = 2 W	—	13.8				$R_{th\,j-h}$ = 31°C/W	stud: 8–32 UNC
	G_p > 6 dB	—	13.8					
	η > 60%	—	13.8					
BLY53	V_{BE} < 1.5 V	0.5	5	C_c = 10 pF	0	13.8	I_{CM} = 4 A	diameter < 10
n-p-n	h_{FE} = 50	0.5	5				V_{CEO} = 18 V	height < 5.8
transmitter	f_T = 800 MHz	0.5	5				P_{tot} = 15 W	leads > 21.7
f.m.	P_i < 2 W	—	13.8				T_j = 200°C	stud length < 12
	P_o = 6 W	—	13.8				$R_{th\,j-h}$ = 12.5°C/W	stud: 8–32 UNC
	G_p > 4.7 dB	—	13.8					
	η > 60%	—	13.8					

radio earth to match the car earth. The Tait T82 had a similar positive/negative earth selector. This feature added considerable complexity to internal circuitry. The T152 solved the positive/negative earth dilemma in a novel way. No chassis switching was required. Upon installation, the chassis would end up connected to vehicle chassis potential via the antenna coax. The chassis was not required to conduct any DC supply current making the chassis connection irrelevant. A red/black cable pair supplied 12VDC directly to the PCB (printed circuit board) via the Red Range connector. For best results this cable pair would be connected directly to the vehicle's 12 volt battery terminals while always observing polarity. The essence of this approach to dual polarity was in holding the PCB negative at a secure RF (radio frequency) ground. This was done by connecting several capacitors between the chassis and PCB negative, spaced at intervals around the periphery. But traditional capacitors introduced too much inductance, adversely affecting the security of the ground. The breakthrough came with the use of feedthrough capacitors, outer soldered directly to chassis and inner soldered directly to the PCB. The application of feedthrough capacitors for this purpose was the brainchild of Angus Tait himself. John often stressed how Angus had been much more than a bystander when the T152 was designed.

The hybrid sets were large, heavy and cumbersome, requiring a two-hand lift. The T152 was shaping up to be small enough and light enough to be easily gripped with one hand. So it made sense that it should slide into a dedicated cradle, engaging a connector when fully home. Once the cradle was installed in a vehicle, the Tait radiotelephone simply slid in, with self-aligning connector engagement. It could then be secured in place by a pair of thumb screws, one each side. Radiotelephones were big ticket items in the day and the ability to share a few units between many cradle equipped vehicles made good economic sense. As new Tait models were added, such as the T162, T172 and T182, all were designed to fit the same cradle. The connector used went by the name: Red Range. It was not unlike a giant version of the Apple Lightning Connector. It measured about 50x20mm

A Red Range connector of the type fitted to the Tait cradle-mounted AM sets. Gold plated contacts in dull red Bakelite-like housing. This example has been fitted with a lamp and was used for testing the integrity of the 12 Volt supply to the cradles.

and was always highly reliable. The only exception was if a set was forced in upside down. This action would split the connector housing in the radiotelephone, resulting in loss of contact pressure which would lead to unreliable connection. But this fault was rare. Of the 16 contacts, two pair at one end were used for 12 volts. An external loudspeaker connected near the middle. At the other end, three side-by-side contacts provided for the antenna, centre pin to coax inner, with the adjacent two connecting to split pigtails of coax braid. This deviation from the ideal presented some discontinuity within the 50 Ohm antenna coax but the effect was tolerable at VHF. A decade after the T152, the UHF T196 required a dedicated coaxial connector and so a D-Sub, with integral antenna connector was chosen. Just as the AM cradle accepted all the AM sets, so too the FM cradle with the D-Sub connector accepted all the FM sets, the T196, T198 and T199 as well as their synthesised counterparts, the T490s. For the T500 series that followed, cost pressures were such that plug-in cradles had to be abandoned, as they were again for the T2000 models.

The frontal aspect of the T152 measured a little over 150mm wide and 50mm high. Length was 280mm. Knobs protruded a further 20mm. After removing a single screw at the rear, the outer sleeve could be slid from the chassis. This very simple disassembly gave full access to both sides of the printed circuit board as can be seen on the cover of this book. The T152 weighed 1.5kg. Total length including cradle and knobs was about 320mm. When the first cell phone arrived in the mid-80s, the Motorola DynaTAC 8000X or "brick", it was large. Two side by side are larger than a T152. Little wonder that the first all transistor Tait product was so successful. But it didn't stop there.

Transmitting transistor packages (here, package does not mean cardboard box but rather, the actual component that is soldered into the printed circuit board) took a few years to evolve into their final shape. From the early 1970s onward, they took the form of a 10mm diameter button having four equally spaced horizontal gold plated copper foil wings and a vertical mounting stud with an American 10-24 thread. If held by the stud, the package resembled a 4-bladed propellor. The later T152 were adapted to accept these parts. The first new design to have one of these packages was the T162, a product similar in performance to the T152 but about 60mm shorter. When I began in 1976, the T162 was the mainstay product. Also in production was the "high band" T172 and 25 Watt T182c. To reliably get 25 Watts, two transmitting transistors were mounted side by side and operated in a circuit configuration known as push-pull. As the "c" suffix would suggest, there had been an earlier T182. This achieved 20 Watts from a single transistor. Because of the demand that 20 Watts placed on the transistor, a protection system that sensed a poor load had to be included to guard against damage which could otherwise result from a broken antenna.

At the years went by, a trend developed where the 20 Watt T182 models would come in for service but appear to function correctly under testing. This was put down to nuisance tripping of the protection circuit. Because transmitting transistors had fallen in price by this time, the protection circuits were disabled. In the event that any real installation problem damaged the transmitter in future, repair would not be expensive. Protection of the 25 Watt 182c was afforded by the combined ruggedness of the dual output transistors.

The aviation band has always used and still does use amplitude modulation, the same modulation method as used on the Tait sets described above. Although the aviation industry might one day change to a sophisticated digital system, AM provides an inadvertent safety feature not offered by FM. A feature of FM (frequency modulation) known as the "capture effect" is usually an advantage. Where two transmissions fall on the same channel, an FM receiver will be captured by the stronger signal and inherently block out the weaker, usually unwanted, transmission. A similar situation in AM will result in the weaker transmission making itself known by causing a "beat" or whistle in the receiver. In uncontrolled airspace, this beat might be the only indication of an as yet unseen aircraft. AM inherently made the Tait products suitable for use on the aviation band. But their compliment of just six channels usually left them as unsuitable for use in aircraft. Even so there was sufficient demand that Tait aviation radiotelephones were designed and built, the first being the T172AV. This had the restriction that its channels had to be clustered within certain frequency limits. A later iteration, the T373, featured a frontend that was tuned by "variable capacitance diodes", giving it the ability to operate over the aviation band of 118 to 136 MHz, but still with the limitation of 6 channels. MOTAT in Auckland have one of these sets in their collection. Searching <motat object 44841> should find it.

From AM to FM

From its earliest days, broadcast radio had utilised a modulation system known as AM (amplitude modulation). Theoretically at least, AM does not provide for the best transmission efficiency but because it allows receivers to employ very simple detectors (the detector circuit translates the radio signal to the audio signal), AM is ideal for broadcast because each inefficient transmitter is received by thousands upon thousands of simple and efficient receivers. AM was also used in the early days of point to point radio communication simply because it was an established technology which sat comfortably within the capabilities of valve circuitry. The advent of the transistor and integrated circuit shifted the economics of point to point radio communication away from AM and towards FM (frequency modulation). Integrated circuits were developed which included IF (intermediate frequency) stages together with the detector to greatly simplify the FM receiver. In FM transmitters, low level transistor circuitry provided the modulation function that had required power transistors and a transformer in their AM counterparts.

Through to the mid-70s, much of New Zealand's radio telephone service used the spectrum either side of 100MHz. This needed to be cleared to free up the 88-108MHz band for high fidelity broadcast radio, as was the standard in many other countries. Further study would be required to find the exact order in which spectrum allocation changed. But in the mid-70s, Tait engineers were developing the company's first FM set, the T193. It was very highly anticipated. It even invited the quip, "Angus might change his initials from AM Tait to FM Tait!" It had the same 6" x 2" frontal aspect as the AM models but was much shorter, making it Tait's smallest set. Rather than utilise a single PCB, as was the norm for Tait transistorised sets, it had two. The transmitter board was fixed in place while the receiver board was hinged for easy access. The T193 was not without its teething problems. In particular the phase modulator was difficult to align. Other problems stemmed from its small size. But it held the fort well until being superseded by the T198.

Most radio telephone services relied on hilltop repeaters. Tait provided the radio equipment for a lot of this infrastructure over the years, through their Field Engineering Division. Equipment for the repeater sites lagged a little behind the development of the mainline products for vehicles. When there was a requirement for FM repeaters, the head of Field Engineering, Charles Dickey, took action. He lifted both the receiver and transmitter sections from the T193 and designed them onto their own circuitboards that were in keeping with other Tait repeater products. This was in the era before CAD, and not only did he do the job single handedly, he did the printed circuit board artworks on his kitchen table. This new configuration suited the T193 circuitry. With the luxury of more space, both the receiver and transmitter circuits worked extremely well.

Hot on the heels of the T193, came the T196, the first UHF set. It retreated from the compact size of the former and instead, matched the dimensions of the AM T162. An optional longer version, having space at the front for ancillary circuit boards, matched the size of the T182. Also FM, the T196 was a clean slate design and had 3 circuit boards. The receiver board was hinge mounted at the bottom and the transmitter board fixed at the top. On the rear, the PA (power amplifier) board sat vertically against an extruded heatsink. A punched opening at one end of this housed the female D-Sub connector which included an integral coaxial connector. It engaged a male connector in the mounting cradle. This arrangement allowed for the antenna connector to be very close to the transmitter output.

Opposite:

Project Management (Illustration courtesy, Joe Fone)

NEW PROJECT
NEXT PROJECT
POLICE SET
PRODUCT SUPPORT
TONE SIGNALLING
NEW A.M.
T196 P.A.
T137
DEAD PROJECTS

"Always zere-if you need it!" The pun referred to the "Handbook of Filter Synthesis" by Anatol I Zverev, an A4 format hardcover of 600 pages. The book with its dull red cover could usually be found within arms' reach of Dave Festing. It contained design tables for all kinds of "LC Networks". These networks, containing inductors (L) and capacitors (C), can be found at the heart of many radio circuits and have always been very difficult to design from the ground up. Zverev contained almost all possible network configurations together with a "seed" value for each component. These seed values, after first being scaled according to frequency and other factors, yielded the final inductance and capacitance values. Dave was fully adept at applying Zverev to transmitter design. The result was adjustment-free transmitter circuitry. Compared to the then existing AM sets, the advantage was clear. After crystals were fitted to the AM sets, both receiver and transmitter required adjustment during the final run-up. But for final run-up of the T196, T198 and T199, little or no adjustment was needed in the transmitter stages. The receivers however, still required the final adjustments.

The UHF T196 receiver used "helical resonators" in its frontend. Although the name sounds foreboding, they are actually mostly air inside, but with a coil connected at one end only and a short brass rod screwed in from the top for frequency adjustment. The invention stems from 1950, relatively late for anything related to radio. The design methodology came even later, being first published in 1967 in the Zverev handbook mentioned above. In the T196, six resonators, arranged in pairs, were incorporated into a single die-cast housing. At about 140mm long, it spanned the width of the receiver board. I remember often seeing these units on John Croft's desk in the early 80s at Manchester St and soon appreciated that John knew them inside out. This technology was, after all, within the domain of the radiotelephone person, John being the quintessential example. But Tait Electronics had excellent production engineers too.

Des Philpott moved from the Moorhouse Ave branch to production engineering in the late 70s and once took the time to show me some of the innovations. The method by which the coils were soldered to the helical resonator housings was exceptionally clever. A full appreciation is worth a trip back in time. In 1960s radio shops, there were three popular types of soldering irons in use. An instant heat soldering gun with built-in low voltage transformer having an on-off trigger in the pistol grip handle and a thick "U" of resistance wire forming the tip. A 65 Watt Solon which was usually left on all day because of its slow warmup time. Finally, the Scope Iron, an Australian invention from the early 1950s. This was an innovative quick-heat design powered from a 3 Volt transformer. The element was a carbon button or rod, 4mm diameter and 6mm in length, set on the end of a spring return pushrod engaged into a Bakelite sliding collar on the handle. Sliding the collar pushed the carbon button onto the base of the short copper soldering tip, completing the electrical circuit and producing concentrated heat at the copper carbon interface. For soldering the helical resonators, just the carbon button and rod were required, the die-cast housing itself being connected to one pole of the 3 Volt transformer and serving as the "tip". When the carbon was manually brought into contact with the housing in the vicinity of the soldering point, instant soldering heat was the result. This made soldering the wire helix into the housing very easy.

Screw-in copper tips and carbon heating elements for Scope Irons.

The T198 high band VHF and T199 low band VHF FM sets quickly followed the T196 and shared much in common, including the intermediate frequency (IF) stage and *noise blanker*. The noise bursts from unsuppressed vehicle ignitions could sometimes cause interference in receivers. Some early AM sets included a suppression circuit involving a series diode designed to briefly turn off for the duration of each noise pulse. This type of circuit, usually placed after the detector, has limited effectiveness due to theoretical reasons. The IF stage includes the bandpass filter which defines a receiver's selectivity, the receiver's ability to reject unwanted adjacent channels. An unfortunate byproduct of a bandpass filter is that it stretches noise pulses according to an unpalatable mathematical function known as the Fourier Transform. The most effective type of noise suppression circuit must be fitted before the bandpass filter, where the pulses have not yet been stretched. It is known as a "noise blanker". A very effective noise blanker circuit was fitted in T196, 8 and 9 sets. It was fitted between the output of the mixer and the input to the xtal filter (crystal filter or aforementioned bandpass filter). In terms of theory, its operation was very complicated but in terms of embodiment, it was quite simple due to the availability of a suitable IC (integrated circuit). Almost a complete receiver in itself, it amplified and detected the output from the mixer and upon sensing each noise pulse would block the direct path from the mixer to the xtal filter. This circuitry required very high internal amplification and developed signal voltages that under normal circumstances would radiate into various parts of the main receiver and recirculate. The masterstroke of the design was the selection of an IC which contained the high level signals within its tiny dimensions thereby eliminating any radiation. A decade later when the T2000 was being developed, this technique for preventing recirculation was somehow forgotten. The very successful T800 basestation designs inspired the T2000 to have multiple compartments cast within a single aluminium chassis. So in the initial circuitboard layout, the noise blanker circuit was relegated to a different compartment from the receiver proper as the next best way to prevent recirculation. Even so, when Angus learned of this he was heard to say, "We've gone backwards!"

A second innovation in the T196, 8 and 9 was the phase modulator. (Although frequency modulation is the end result, it is often generated via phase modulation together with the application of a simple mathematical process, requiring a capacitor, in the audio circuit.) The phase modulator in

An off-cut of the extrusion used for the T196 etc heatsinks. The thin section at left made for easy punching of the D-Sub connector opening.

the first Tait FM product, the T193, had been difficult to align. Although this problem faded as technicians refined their tuning techniques, the phase modulators in the T196 etc required no alignment at all. This achievement was due to two factors. For the T193 transmitter, modulation applied at the crystal frequency was multiplied by a factor of just three, placing high demands upon the modulating circuit and forcing the use of tuned circuits. But for the T196 etc, a higher multiplication was chosen, allowing the use of fixed value active circuits in the modulator. To quote Ray Vickers, an engineering manager at that time, "You just put the parts in the circuitboard and it works"

Up until the arrival of the T490 synthesised sets, all Tait radiotelephones required one pair of xtals, (quartz crystals) for each channel. One defined the receiver frequency and the other, the transmitter frequency. The circuitboards of most sets could accommodate up to 12 xtals, for up to 6 channel capability. Quartz crystals are exactly as the same suggests. A slither of quartz set between two electrodes. Quartz is piezoelectric, meaning that it will vibrate in sympathy with an electrical signal applied to the electrodes. But when a xtal is connected into an oscillating circuit, the opposite applies. The oscillator circuit "invites" the slither of quartz to vibrate at its own resonant frequency. The slither's resonant frequency is in turn determined by its exact size. During manufacture, the tiny slithers of quartz are ground and/or etched until the desired frequency is arrived at.

Xtals were not made in-house but by any of several New Zealand suppliers. The reason for xtals in this application is frequency stability. During the life of the component, some surface debris might be shed and cause the frequency to rise very slightly due the lower vibrating mass, but other than that, xtals are renowned for their frequency stability. They do however, change a little with temperature. For the FM sets, particularly the T196, frequency stability requirements over the operating temperature range were beyond the capabilities of the native xtal. To this problem a Tait engineer devised a unique solution. More precisely, a unique form of temperature compensation. He began by developing a specific understanding of what happened within the xtal. From this he devised how to reverse the xtal's temperature dependence using no more than a temperature dependent resistor network connected to the xtal's terminals. Previously it had been assumed that only capacitance or inductance could influence a xtal's frequency.

I was once in John Crofts office at Manchester St with a third person that I cannot remember discussing a topic that I can't remember either. When I made my contribution to the conversation, the other two looked questionably and one asked, "Who told you that?" Given their doubt I became reluctant to implicate my source and said, "A certain engineer." The pair laughed and one immediately responded, "You mean, a VERY certain engineer." They were of course referring to Den. The major innovations described above, noise blanker, phase modulator and xtal temperature compensation were the brainchild of one individual. Dennis Chapman had the ability to begin from nowhere and build up a thorough understanding of a concept. From there, he could always design circuitry based on what he had learned, his designs always working well. But it gets better. Den was always able to articulate his understanding to others in a way that left no doubt about how things worked. Hence, "very certain engineer"! In the mid-1980s, he took his unique skill set away and applied it to switchmode power supplies for the telecom sector. His original designs immediately found favour and along with business partners, he built the company, Eltec changing to Swichtec, into a multimillion dollar affair. They decided to sell up, sometime around the y2k. With a mind freed, Den was able to reapply. He reinvented power electronics for the second time and repeated history with a company named Enatel. But back in 1980, Den was still working hard at Tait.

The chapter, Moorhouse Ave, describes the final run up process involving the fitting of crystals, where one pair was needed for each channel. The technique of frequency synthesis allowed a single crystal, known as the "reference crystal" and fitted during manufacturing, to fulfil the same requirement. The core of frequency synthesis is the VCO or Voltage Controlled Oscillator. This generates the desired frequency, but it is the control loop that it is immersed in that forces it to do so. A "digital fraction" of the VCO's output frequency is compared to a fraction of the reference crystal frequency. The difference between these two frequencies generates the control voltage which is fed back to the VCO, keeping it locked onto the desired frequency. For each channel, a pair of digital codes, one for receive and another for transmit, sets the "digital fraction" referred to above. (Mechanically minded people may prefer to think of clockwork gear ratios where the digital code sets the number of teeth.) The synthesised versions of the T196, T198 and T199 were designed by Den and denoted T496, T498 and T499 respectively. The heavy digital processing involved, demanded the use of purpose designed integrated circuits. At Tait Electronics it had always been preferred to use components that were available from multiple suppliers. But for frequency synthesisers, generic parts did not exist. Because Motorola were a reliable supplier, their ICs were chosen. The way in which the main IC generated the control voltage was a little awkward however. Den soon mastered this and designed a very effective and simple dual speed circuit. The same circuit was used in the later T500 family of products.

In the T490s, the digital codes were stored on an ultraviolet erasable EPROM (erasable programmable recall only memory). This needed a dedicated programmer, the first of which was designed at Manchester St. It was hardware based and quite large, being about the size of an encyclopaedia. A second generation programmer was designed after the move to Wairakei Rd. It was microprocessor based and about the size of a novel. For the T500 series that followed the T490s, a manual approach that required technicians to cut and/or solder links on a removable circuitboard module was adopted for the digital codes. For both the T490s and the T500 series, a final run up was still required. What was gained was that a pair of crystals did not have to be ordered first. The T2000 series, designed either side of 1990 took the final step. This did not need a final run up. Transmitter circuits were broadband, meaning that they worked equally well at any frequency within the product's advertised frequency range. The receiver frontend, instead of using mechanically varying inductors or capacitors, used variable capacitance diodes whose capacitance varies with applied DC voltage. The T2000s were the first Tait products to be microprocessor controlled. The digital codes for the synthesiser were stored in the microprocessor's memory along with the DC voltage values to be applied to the variable capacitance diodes. Instead of the final run up, configuration of T2000 series radiotelephones was by a laptop computer, temporarily connected in place of the plug-in microphone.

Field Engineering

In the 1970s and 80s, the main network of repeater systems up and down New Zealand was provided and maintained by the Post Office, then still government owned. All the receiving and transmitting equipment used in these repeater systems was sourced from New Zealand suppliers wherever possible and Tait offered a good range of suitable products. But New Zealand, being scarcely populated, had many remote areas out of range of the repeater networks which tended to be focussed around cities. Local businesses and other groups often responded by setting up their own repeater systems. This is where the Field Engineering division came in. By mixing and matching the standard range of Tait's purpose designed infrastructure equipment with Field engineering designed parts, stand-alone repeaters were easily constructed. The simplest consisted of a receiver, transmitter and power supply, all mounted in a metal cabinet with hinged door. Cabinets measured about 600mm wide, 300mm high and half a metre front to back. The standard finish was deep green semigloss, slightly lighter than the colour of pine trees. The colour of some of the equipment was colloquially known as "straw". In their most basic form, the connection of mains power and two antennae, one for receive and the other for transmit, completed the installation. Where mains supply was unreliable, a 12 Volt battery would be added into the system, the standard Tait power supply being able to both power the equipment and keep the battery fully charged. Mountain sites often omitted the power supply and relied on a solar panel to keep the battery charged. Solar panels were still very rare and expensive in the 1970s but were much more practical and reliable than the alternative, an autostart generator. The solar panels would continue to charge the batteries even under cloud and deep snow. They had to. Often there was no access to these mountain sites during the winter months. The more complex small repeater systems were sometimes connected to telephone lines. The department manager, Charles

Dickey, had an exceptionally good grounding in all things telephone. In addition to that he covered all the bases in electronics, including radio, audio and digital.

When I began at Field Engineering, early in 1978 from memory, I always thought of the company founder as Mr Tait and had seen him in the distance just a few times. He often mixed with his staff at the local Cokers Pub a few doors north along Manchester St. I was never a regular pub goer as I found the cigarette smoke too unpleasant. My father had told me of the "6 o'clock swill" where patrons rushed from their employment to their local on their way home, and how you gave the right change to the person in front of you and watched it pass from hand to hand to the barman after which your seven-ounce beer was passed all the way back, or at least most of it. October 1967 saw the introduction of 10 o'clock closing, a side effect of which was the booze barn. These were hall sized pubs with small dance floors and loud pop bands adding deafening noise to the suffocating smoke. Carpets absorbed and evaporated so much spilt beer that residues would stick to your shoes with every step, only releasing the floor covering after being lifted an inch. Fortunately, there were still the "local" type pubs without the bands where the air thinned when the crowds departed. One such evening I had the good fortune to be at Cokers among just a few, to listen to a fishing story. It was common knowledge that Mr Tait enjoyed jet boating and in later years it would not be unusual for his boat to be parked in unused space in the Tait Wairakei Rd premises. I can't remember how the subject came up but he began by stating that he'd never had an interest in fishing and went on to describe his one attempt. Mr Tait described how, before embarking on one of his jet boat trips, a fisherman friend had been very insistent that he should borrow his rod and kit and give it a go. Mr Tait described how he accepted the offer and placed the fishing tackle in the back of the boat and headed away. He then started to describe the confusion he experienced and began to gesture a length between the thumb and finger of one hand. When he got to his destination he explained, he went to retrieve the fishing rod only to notice that there were just a few inches of line remaining on the reel. A quick look found that during the rough trip with all the bouncing around, the hook had found its way into the engine compartment with the result that the entire contents of the reel ended up wrapped around the driveshaft. Mr Tait shared our laughter.

The Field Engineering department was situated on the ground floor at 30 Manchester St on the south side of the building in the area beyond the foyer. A side door exited onto a car parking area beside Eaton Place. Perhaps at this time or perhaps a year or two later it was not unusual to see a green EV Fiat Bambina parked here among other cars belonging to the staff. Yes a Fiat 500 EV circa 1980, the brainchild of Dennis Chapman. Peter May recalls, "I helped Den re-power his [Fiat 500] and his instructions to the spray painter and panel-beater (the father of one of our school mates) was to paint it the same colour as the council rubbish bins! The DC motor I sourced from the Mechanic at CWF Hamilton's, a nominally rated 3HP from the early electric milk floats used in Christchurch. Den added fan cooling and managed to get close to the peak HP of a standard Fiat 500 (18HP). The back seat and under the front (where the fuel tank used to be) were filled with traction lead acid batteries needing an extra leaf in the front suspension. The lasting memories I had from driving it was the difference in current (a moving coil meter on the dash) draw on chip seal, compared to road carpet and when he drove out to see me in Lincoln from his house in Sockburn, he had to put it on charge before he could make it home!" Dennis designed and built the necessary electronic control circuitry that allowed the accelerator pedal to regulate the torque from the motor. I did not see it myself, but his colleagues played a nice prank one day. They took the pattern of the wind-up key of a child’s toy, made a scaled up version of it and attached it to the rear of the car! Possibly before the EV, I once saw Dennis walking across the carpark to the side door through rare Christchurch snow, still wearing jandals as always. It would be true to say that I got to know the jandals before I got to know the person. A year or two later, after the move upstairs, I once flicked some excess solder from my iron onto the old wooden floor. A moment later a jandal clad foot landed on the same spot. “Hey, that’s malicious that is”, said Dennis from behind a warm hearted grin.

In the ground floor setting, Charles Dickey and his offsider Chris Chao occupied offices. Chris had come to New Zealand from Singapore to complete his schooling here. We all enjoyed listening to his stories of being a high school student a decade and a half earlier. It was the era of the Elvis inspired brushed back hair. Chris explained how he and all his high school mates carried combs in their back pockets and that if they were out and caught their reflection in a window or shiny car, they would immediately reach for their combs and perfect their hair! Also, we were always interested to hear snippets of Chris’ home country. He once told how his mother was to lose a corner of her land to a motorway project and that Singapore allowed for land to be taken for public works without compensation. Where owners stubbornly refused to release ownership of their land, the road would proceed anyway with the owner having to cover all future maintenance costs for that area of road crossing their land. He was always a starter for a budget meat and three veg meal up town if time permitted during the lunch break and on one occasion taught a few of us how to use chop sticks when Asian dining. Chris had a bench in his office complete with tools, soldering iron and test equipment. He was equally at home running up a radiotelephone or liaising with customers about their system requirements. Field Engineering’s main work area, adjacent Chris’ office, was usually staffed by three technicians, Joe Fone being the mainstay. Across Eaton Place and a few doors further south on Manchester St, there was a dairy with a narrow and poorly lit interior that somehow seemed to suit the thin middle aged shopkeeper. On the counter there was a mechanical cash register of the type where fingers behind glass popped up as the keys were pushed down. On this cash register, the popup fingers still displayed pounds, shillings and pence, even though New Zealand had used decimal currency for a decade. A favourite Field Engineering snack from this dairy was the Whittaker’s Peanut Slab, particularly for Joe and me. Usually these were eaten shiny side up but on one occasion, a small moth was noticed stuck dead centre in the underside. The dairy willingly provided a replacement, but we all used to reminisce and laugh at how I ate as much as possible from around the moth before taking it back to the dairy for a free replacement. Every time the story was retold, it had me getting even closer to the moth! In addition to the electronic work benches, there was some mechanical equipment such as bench grinder and drill press. During the heyday of the building, this area must have been associated with records, mail and money, for at the end was a walk-in safe, about 3 metres long and 2 metres wide. In the time of Field Engineering, it served as a very convenient store room. On one occasion, a very dedicated technician sought to etch a printed circuit board late one afternoon, finishing it just before lockup time. In cleaning up, he emptied the ferric chloride etchant from the etching bath into the first empty vessel he saw and put it out of harm's way in the middle of the safe's concrete floor. In the morning there was a large yellow/brown stain. The etching solution had eaten through the bottom of the old treacle tin!

Volume production of printed circuit boards was well catered for by the many manufacturers throughout New Zealand. At the other end of the scale, one-off boards could be etched after first drawing or painting over the areas where the copper was to be retained, with an etchant resist such as heavily applied felt pen. For intermediate quantities, the Field Engineering management had devised a very effective process. Actual sized artworks were made in the usual way, by applying very narrow self-adhesive tapes and doughnuts, made for the purpose by Bishop Graphics, to transparent Mylar sheet. The next steps were optical. For these, the essential piece of equipment was an ultraviolet (UV) light box. This looked like a tall A4 scanner but with no more than an ultraviolet lamp deep below the glass. Because all the films and resists used were sensitive only to ultraviolet light and not to ambient office lighting, there was no need for a darkroom. The first step of the process was to make a negative using a contact process. The artwork was placed on the glass with the negative film on top of it, the lid closed and the UV lamp turned on for a number of seconds as controlled by a time switch. The developing process involved no more than wiping the exposed negative with developer soaked cotton wool. Where the UV light had passed through the Mylar and exposed the negative film, the developer had no effect. Where the UV light had been blocked by the Bishop tapes on the artwork, the negative film remained unexposed and was simply washed away by the developer, leaving the unexposed areas transparent. The next step involved single sided printed circuit board that had been pre-coated with a UV sensitive resist layer during its manufacture. The negative was placed on the glass of the UV light box and the UV sensitive printed circuit board placed on top. After exposure, developer washed away all the areas of the resist where the negative had blocked the UV, to reveal bare copper. The end result was that the areas where the copper remained covered by the resist layer matched the Bishop tapes pattern of the artwork. The board was then etched with ferric chloride in the usual way, after which the remaining resist could be washed away with an appropriate solvent. The very last step was to drill the holes for the component leads, the artwork having been prepared in such a way as to result in tiny holes in the copper, which marked the points to be drilled. With this method, a printed circuit board could be designed, etched, assembled and tested all in the same day.

The same UV light box was also used for the Scotchcal process. This involved thin self-adhesive A4 sized aluminium sheets coated with a durable emulsion, black and red being kept in stock. First an actual size artwork was prepared with all the required lettering and other graphical features. This was placed on the glass of the UV light box and then the Scotchcal placed on top. After exposure, developer-soaked cotton wool washed away the areas where the artwork had blocked the UV light. The end result was a black panel with all the lettering and other features appearing in shiny anodised aluminium. Between printed circuit boards and Scotchcal, very professional looking one-off units were easily constructed. But occasionally, offcuts of Scotchcal found other uses. During this era, there were many interesting car stickers. A favourite of

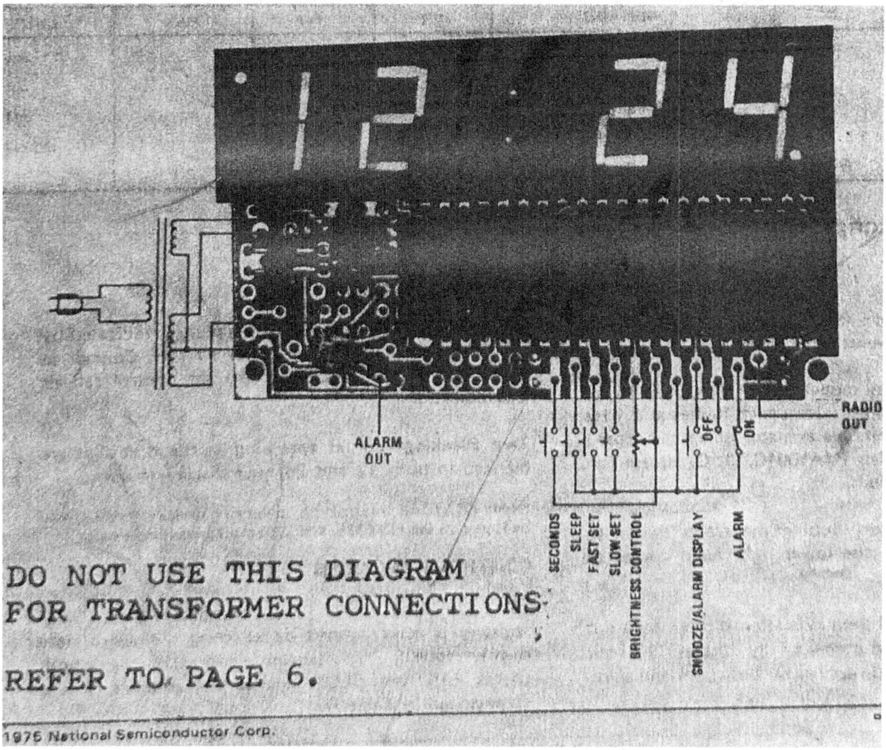

Photograph of part an old photocopy of the MA1001 digital clock module data sheet. It serves to illustrate how photocopy quality deteriorates when each successive copy becomes the next master. Lines are intact but almost all detail has been lost from the image.

teachers, "Education Cuts Don't Heal". Then there were "Save the Whales", tigers, lions, elephants, animals all in sundry in fact. Then "Support Trade Unions", support this activist group, support that activist group, support this political prisoner, support that hunger striker. It all possessed one technician to turn to red Scotchcal. His bumper sticker read: Support Apathy.

So long as it didn't get in the way of work flows, the management were accommodating of home projects, the view being that the experience was always beneficial to the employee. One day a technician brought a car radio to work in the hope its problem might benefit from group think.

Three or four of us puzzled over it through lunch time. But the task lingered on after the end of the break. Next thing our manager, Charles Dickey, appeared. For many bosses, "Back to work." would have been the stern warning. But not Charles. His approach was different, "Haven't you guys got that car radio fixed yet?" he jokingly accused. He then gently ushered us aside and took over. He had it fixed in ten minutes while we watched on. It was a sign of an agile mind, one instantly able to switch from the long distance thinking of management to the here and now of fault finding. Another instance of his abilities was a timing system for some ski races in Canterbury. He used the Tait 3-tone system over a radiotelephone channel. The start gate sent a unique three tone sequence that initiated an electronic stopwatch situated in the race officials' hut. The finish gate sent a different three tone sequence that halted the stopwatch. Another project undertaken around that same time involved a gesture of charity. An existing system involving a pair of keyboards and displays allowed for text to be transmitted via telephones and offered a means of communication for the deaf community. Charles had previously ordered a selection of specialist audio integrated circuits from an English company. With one of these, together with a microphone, I built a circuit that responded to a telephone's bell. Charles instructed an electrician on how to link this into the lighting circuits of a house's switchboard so that when the phone rang, lights flickered out with each ring of the bell, something noticeable even during the daylight hours. But the most complicated project of the late 70s was one for a government department in Wellington. It had offices in several locations around the city and required point to point radio communication between them. In addition to voice, the system was required to convey various types of signalling protocols. Much of the equipment for this ancillary requirement was made in-house and involved much point to point wiring in standard Tait metalwork. Joe Fone took command of this. His work was so precise and neat that these units became the hallmark of the Field Engineering art at that time, being proudly displayed by Charles Dickey or Chris Chao to every visitor.

The standard Tait metalwork was popular for home projects. Here a National Semiconductor MA1001 digital clock module gets a professional looking finish. Red digits and buttons on black with chrome escutcheon and handle.

The standard Tait metalwork of the T152 lent itself very well to many applications outside the original purpose. For basestation use it was oriented so that the front panel sat vertically, allowing 7 or sometimes 8 such units to be arranged horizontally across the shelf of a 19 inch rack, the addition of a wide "U" shaped handle aiding unplugging. In situations where special test equipment was not commercially available and had to be made, this same metalwork was always chosen. Although not always strictly necessary, the U handle was often retained to provide some bump protection to sensitive adjustments on the front panel. One important piece of test equipment was the frequency counter, as it was needed when setting a radiotelephone's crystals exactly to the channel frequency. Most of the German made Schomandl FD1 frequency meters had been retired by the mid-1970s, the new favourite being a digital frequency counter from Galbraith. These New Zealand made units, also available in kit set form, had the characteristic orange Nixie tube indicators displaying the digits. The Galbraith were reliable and accurate, but quite large and soon upstaged by a unit from SALCOM, or Sea, Air and Land COMmunication. This company was established by three Tait employees, Charles Dickey, Colin McKenzie and John Croft in 1975. The idea was that Salcom would offer solutions in niche areas that a company the size of Tait would struggle to do economically. The frequency counter was an example in point. Tait could not have afforded the distraction of having to design a digital frequency counter. On the other hand, Salcom would have struggled to attain attractive metalwork given their low production numbers. The solution? A frequency counter in standard Tait metalwork. Charles had designed a nice product with all components assembled on a single printed circuit board. Power supply devices were distributed around the chassis so as to avoid any concentration of heat. It took up little room on the technician's bench and the red 7-segment LED display was easy to read. It was always exciting to get any piece of newly released test equipment, but this was extra special. All the while, the Field Engineering expertise continued to draw in new customers, with radio links for the NZED (New Zealand Electricity Department) in Twizel being made at this time.

Most hydro schemes had involved the building of dams to create artificial lakes. For the Twizel scheme, three natural lakes pre-existed and so were interconnected with dozens of kilometres of canals. The end result was that 18 imperial gallons (82 litres) of water flowing from Lake Tekapo, through the Twizel scheme and then on and down through the three Waitaki hydro dams would make enough electricity to boil your electric jug. So stated a sign in the Twizel visitor centre at that time. Other information referred to the very high accuracy required for the surveying of the canals. The fall was required to be extremely precise so that the body of water would flow at a uniform speed, about walking pace, for the entire length of each canal. SCADA (Supervisory Control And Data Acquisition) was a buzzword of the era and because the Twizel scheme was so spread out, data had to be relayed over long distances. Tait provided the ideal system for the data pipelines using a system known as hot standby. All the radio links were duplicated in their entirety, one being active and the other standing by. Any glitch would cause the active and standby channels to automatically switch places, resulting in extremely reliable data transmission. The system was complex even by Field Engineering standards and I remember Ian Gardiner of Engineering proper being involved.

Sometime between late 1978 and mid-ish 1979, Field Engineering moved up to the third floor of the Manchester St building, to a location beside the engineering division which was simply known as "the lab". From late 1979 to late 1980, I took leave without pay and went to Campbell Island to work as a DSIR technician. I returned to the same place but to some different faces, including a tall American. Fred was ex navy and had served in the US nuclear submarine fleet. We were interested to compare our experiences, Fred among dozens of crew in the confinements of an iron hull for three months at a time and me, one of less than a dozen on an island for a year. Fred obviously had limits on what he could tell and to many questions that seemed innocuous he would clam and say, "Sorry, that's classified." Around this time the feature movie Goodbye Pork Pie was released. I don't remember anyone claiming it to be one of the great movies but it was New Zealand made and quite entertaining. Many of us went to see it at various times and I remember a colleague had said that in one Christchurch scene, Tait's Kaiapoi building was visible in the background, standing out due to the antennae on the roof. The feeders, or wires of coaxial cable, for many of these antennae were routed to a panel of connectors on the south wall of the lab. It must have been during a lunch break, because there were not many people about, that a sharp "crack" caught my attention. I looked, saw nothing and thought no more of it. Then another "crack". I got up and walked toward where the sound had come from. On the third or fourth crack, I saw the associated spark jumping across one of the antenna connectors on the wall. A "sleeve dipole" antenna on the roof was collecting static electricity from the atmosphere. The other connectors on the panel did not exhibit the same effect due to their antenna designs shorting out any static buildup. I looked around and called the few people I saw to come and watch. Tens of thousands of volts would have been required to jump the gap across the connector. As we watched, the sparks appeared with increasing rapidity, eventually striking a few times a second. Next we heard a subdued thunderclap. So ended the sparks, as if a lightning strike had discharged the sky. Our day's entertainment had ended.

Another significant project was in the works in 1981, or more specifically, the Morrinsville Waterworks. Their existing system could monitor a reservoir level and perform a few other simple functions over their radiotelephone channel. It was very sophisticated for its era, circa 1960. It transmitted a sequence of tones, the exact sequence being determined by a float level within the reservoir. Tones were generated by vibrating reeds, each together with its electromagnetic actuator sealed in its own plug-in unit about 20mm diameter and 120mm long. The receiving unit at the office detected the tones with resonant circuits, each tone sequence illuminating its own pattern of lamps from which the staff could glean water level. Another function of the office unit was to interrogate the reservoir unit by transmitting its own pair of tones, one following the other. The staff out on the job had learned how to shortcut some of this. The tones could be heard from all the radiotelephones in the vehicle fleet. By listening, they learnt how to mentally decode the sequence into a water level. It was said that some of the more musical staff could initiate the sequence by whistling the interrogation tones into their radiotelephone's microphone. The Morrinsville council operated their own fleet vehicle service workshop as was usual for government and municipal departments of the day. There, one particular mechanic had a musical spanner and when a colleague was making a radiotelephone call, he would throw the spanner onto the concrete floor whereupon its ringing sound would mimic the interrogation tones, initiating the reservoir sequence and interrupting the radiotelephone voice traffic. Altogether the Morrinsville system was quite outdated and Field Engineering was able to offer a futuristic solution.

During the installation, two junior plumbers were pondering the water pressure at a particular point in the Morrinsville Water Treatment Plant. Peter Squires suggested the rule of thumb, "half a pound per square inch for every foot of head". The response was as if a referee's decision had gone against their home rugby team, "N-a-a-a-h-h-h", meaning: what would this tekkie know about plumbing? Peter simply said, "cubic foot of water, 62.5 pounds spread over 12*12=144 square inches." There was a stunned silence. The TMO (television match official) decision was final and undeniable. Peter was an immensely practical member of the academic staff at the Engineering School of the University of Canterbury. In about 1976, for the AM sets, he had designed a new "audio compressor", the circuit that caused the same uniform voice level to be transmitted independently of how loudly or quietly the person spoke or how far away from the microphone. It was now 1981 and Peter designed the

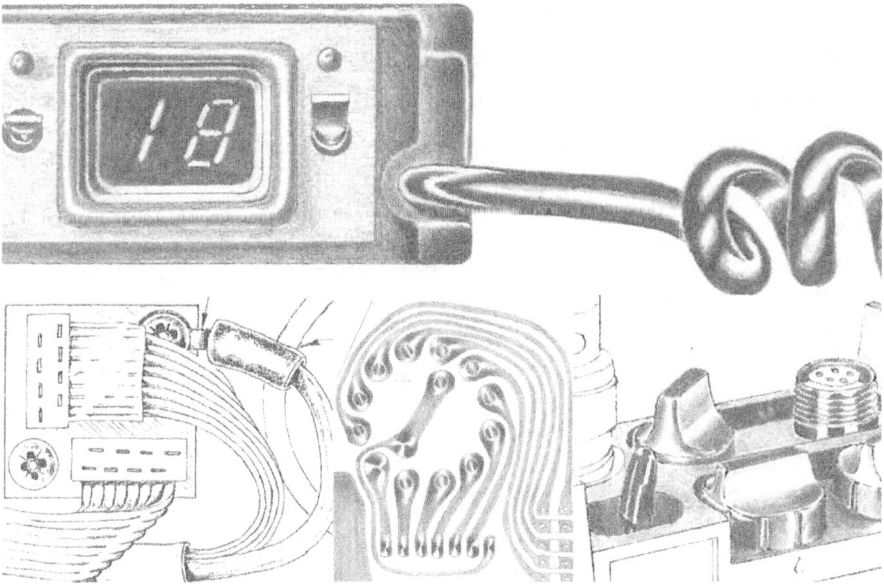

Examples of Joe Fone's drawing skills. Contrary to photographs, each photocopy of these drawings could become the next master, over and over again and image quality still keep its utility. This is in total contrast to the clock module example a few pages up. Images courtesy, Joe Fone.

sophisticated telemetry system for Morrinsville. All the radio links were of course Tait, as were various of the ancillary devices and the metalwork into which Peter's microprocessor equipped circuitboards were fitted. The home unit provided all the control and monitoring functions for the various pump stations, water treatment plant, reservoir and, where required, hard copy was available via the incorporated 60mm wide printer. All the remote equipment was housed in the standard green cabinets.

At about this time, Field Engineering was beginning not to exist. Engineering proper had been split three ways into handhelds, basestations and mobiles. In addition to receivers and transmitters, the basestation group was designing various ancillary units for production which allowed the more adventurous of the service branches and dealers to design their own repeaters through a mix and match of standard parts from the Tait catalogue. Charles Dickey had transitioned almost totally to Salcom and soon Chris Chao would move to Deltec, the antenna designer and manufacturer in Wellington. Joe Fone's artistic skills were impossible for the drawing office to ignore and I happened to be at the right place at the right time to fill a gap in the handheld group. Other technicians moved to different positions within the company.

The Handhelds

When I was at Campbell Island in 1980, radio news reported a light plane crash, rare in NZ then, as they thankfully remain today. The name of a survivor caught my attention. John Croft. I couldn't be sure because John's age was reported as 30s whereas I'd imagined him to be early 40s. But when I returned to Tait Electronics at the beginning of 1981, I learned that it had indeed been John, designer of the T152. In spite of this, he had got the UHF FM handheld, the T303, into production. Although it was the second UHF product made by Tait, miniaturisation demanded a significant departure from the T196, especially in the receiver. It reverted to dual conversion as had been the case for the hybrid sets. This had been made possible by a new integrated circuit from Motorola that included most of the receiver, including the second mixer. The other main difference was in the construction of the frontend. Helical resonators were used, but they had to be much smaller than those in the T196.

When duty free Japanese transistor radios arrived in NZ in the early 1960s, the view inside wowed, not just with the miniaturisation, but with the precision of it. Although wires, resistors and capacitors were often higgledy-piggledy, the shielding cans were not only tiny, but beautifully and accurately made. The T152 design included some of these components, made by Toko in Japan. In the cover photograph, these are the smallest of the shiny square cans, measuring 10x10mm and having what looks like a black screw head below the hole in the top. Empty cans such as these became the basis for the T303 helical resonators. A threaded brass insert was affixed to the top and the adjustable brass plug screwed into it. The modified cans together with the helix coils were mounted on the circuitboard in the usual way. The YouTube video 9MKsZrFanC0 features two scenes with this receiver, one at 17 seconds and the other at 1:18, the helical resonators being the three pairs of cans with brass screws. The presenter in the video is of course Ian Gardener who features in both the "last 8" and "first 12" photographs (page viii). In addition to his impressive career at Tait, Ian was an experienced tramper and mountaineer and I remember once asking him about food rationing before embarking on a Fiordland trip with some friends. About one and a half pounds per day per person with dry biscuits a good staple he suggested. He was heavily involved with the Arthur's Pass National Park in the days before it fell under DOC administration. By the early 80s, some of the trampers' huts had radiotelephones installed for communication, via a repeater, with the Park HQ in Arthur's Pass village. I remember once

A T307 handheld prototype with its battery pack dropped into the dedicated one hour charger having missing faceplate. When thumb operation of the original flat knobs proved to be impractical, tall knobs were introduced.

being invited along with John Croft to see if the repeater could be accessed from the Summit Road with a VHF handheld. From memory, line of sight distance was 80 miles and the objective was to try different types of antennae. All antennae gave contact, with an impractically long quarter wave whip working best.

John didn't begin as a radiotelephone person. He had come through the NZED (New Zealand Electricity Department) and told stories of hanging in a cage under the DC line during its early days. He described how leaving one pylon was easy but hauling the cage toward the next one kept getting harder as the cage got closer. The DC line is the transmission line that brings electricity from where it is generated in the Waitaki and Clutha hydro schemes, up through the South Island and under Cook Strait to Haywards where it is converted back to AC for consumption throughout the North Island. John described how relative to ground, there was a positive line and a negative line having equal and opposite currents, with any imbalance having to flow through the ground and resulting in higher transmission losses. Another experience with the NZED had involved monitoring transformer temperatures when, during a disruption to the South Island grid, Christchurch was being supplied from Lake Coleridge. John began with A M Tait Ltd in the mid to late 60s. He did have some involvement with the Century Series during its troubled entry into service but then worked fully on the T152. He was very humble about this achievement. In fact, most Tait engineers were the same. Their focus was always on their current objective to the point that they didn't dwell on the past. But fortunately, every now and then, something in a conversation would trigger a memory. Although, perhaps there were more words devoted to jokes than to the past. EG. A boy named Mark was sent out to check the letterbox in the dead of night because he forgot during the day. As he began the walk down the driveway, he became aware of rustling in the adjacent hedge. Then, "Mark, Mark." He froze. The disturbance ceased. Slowly Mark began to creep, ever so quietly toward the letterbox. He was almost there when, "MARK… Mark, Mark, Mark." He jumped the last few steps, grabbed the mail and sprinted for the house. He was almost home when again, "MARK, MARK". He stood motionless as a dark shadow emerged. As it moved toward him, it entered the beam of a distant streetlight and Mark saw what it was. A hair-lipped dog! But by far the most conversation was devoted to the job at hand with every now and again, an insight into something rarely thought about.

At the polytechnic or university, a rule going by the name *Maximum Power Transfer Theorem* was regularly taught along with its mathematical proof. Conditions within a radio circuit or along a telephone line were usually arranged accordingly. A consequence of going by this rule was that power was wasted at the sending end, the wasted power and delivered power being of equal measure. This loss, as proven by the theorem, was always accepted as a fact of life. John was able to point out, with reasoning not requiring mathematics, that sometimes it was best not to abide by the Maximum Power Transfer Theorem. He began using the electricity grid as an example, pointing out that to be beholden to the theorem, the generators would have to waste as much power as NZ consumed. The absurdity was proof that the maximum power transfer theorem need not always apply. John then invoked the case of a radio transmitter. According to the theorem, a transmitter with 25 Watts of output would have to waste another 25 Watts in its output transistor, clearly an undesirable situation. Again, the Maximum Power Transfer Theorem does not apply to radio transmitters. This kind of insight extended to accepting humour too, John becoming the victim of a prank I learned of only recently. Referring again to the T303 in the museum video above, it concerns the thin retaining cord on the ancillaries connector cover. Peter May tells the story: I recall a John Croft trick that Lisle Hood played. He had found a fine black cord for retaining a connector covering cap to the hand held. John was in one of those Senior Engineer offices alongside the lab with a big window, at the woollen mill building in Manchester Street and he was known to turn up a bit hungover and sleepy, a bit later than everyone else. Lisle tied John's telephone hand set to the phone with this fine cord and then gathered everyone together to watch when John came in to work, then called him. In his poor state he picked up the whole phone and put it to his ear. It had us in fits for some time.

Up until the handheld, the construction of Tait products had been largely from sheet metal, with knobs and front panel escutcheons being the main exception. A handheld product with removable battery pack together with a dedicated charger was beyond sheet metal. The decision was taken to go with a third party housing from Asia. Although this had larger dimensions than competing product, the plastic battery pack would comfortably fit ten AA NiCad cells. Two NZ made circuitboards, one for transmitter and the other for receiver, could be accommodated within the die-cast frame, under plastic outer covers. All the electronic circuitry, including battery charger, was designed and built by Tait. As the market began to flourish, the need for a multiway charger emerged. Batteries could be charged whether attached to the bottom of the handheld or not and were simply dropped into a recess, or rectangular bucket, in the one-hour fast-charger. The bucket assembly was available without the usual integral charger body and several buckets were arranged in line in New Zealand made metalwork to form the multi charger. My first task for John was to shrink the printed circuit board to suit the internal dimensions of the new multi-charger. My first experience making printed circuits had been as a schoolboy hobbyist, using ferric chloride etchant and white Fascinac shoe paint as the etchant resist. For production artworks, black tapes known as Bishops Graphics were applied at twice full size onto transparent sheet. In those days, this was what the Printed Circuit Board Manufacturer worked from. When the smaller charger prototype circuitboards were made and tested, their performance matched the original larger boards. As T303 ancillary products were forming up, such as separately available batteries, two types of charger and a leather case, it was time for the next step. A VHF handheld, the T302.

The T302 had much in common with the T303, the main exceptions being the transmitter and frontend of the receiver. John designed the receiver frontend and Dave Festing the Transmitter. The phase modulator took up more circuitboard area than its counterpart in the T303, resulting in the final transmitting transistor having to move closer to the antenna socket and out of reach of a heat-sinking bracket. This was a New Zealand made addition to the Asian made chassis. It was as simple as a postage stamp sized piece of copper sheet having three holes and three bends. But it was "hard tooled", meaning that considerable upfront investment had been required. A new bracket to suit the new transistor position would require a repeat investment. Could there be another way? "Could you possibly have a go at the printed circuit board layout with the objective of moving the final transmitting transistor?" I was asked. At a glance, it looked almost possible. After a few days with pencil, rubber and graph paper, it looked probable. It is always desirable in manufacturing to have commonality between similar models. After re-laying the VHF transmitter circuitry, both the T303 and T302 were able to use the same heat-sinking bracket in the same location. These handhelds shared some interesting manufacturing techniques too. These were demonstrated to me by Des Philpott whom I'd previously known at the Moorhouse Ave Branch. The battery packs were assembled in-house, with interconnections being made by metal straps which were spot welded to the battery caps. Spot welder electrodes usually approach the job, one from the top and the other from the bottom, ridiculous in this situation. The solution was to place the two electrodes side by side. This resulted in two side by side welds, one under each electrode, with the welding current flowing horizontally in the battery cap to complete the circuit. Another commonality between the handheld models was the shapes of the receiver and transmitter circuitboards. Today, PCB manufacturers have computer controlled cutting technology, but in 1970s New Zealand, nonuniform shapes were trimmed to final size in dedicated profile punches. Usually the PCB manufacturer performed this step and supplied the boards in their finished shape. For the handhelds, both the receiver board and the transmitter board were small and flimsy and because of this, they were supplied as a pair, still embedded within the larger PCB panel from which they would later be punched. All the assembly and soldering functions were performed while the pair of circuitboards remained part of the larger panel, profile punching being the final step. The profile punch was located within the assembly line and including its integral table, was about the size of an old treadle sewing machine. Two accurately drilled holes in the panel slid over two dowel pins, to give accurate location. The punch mechanism was driven by compressed air. The force required by the punch required a piston area beyond the size of practicality. A novel solution was found. A wheelbarrow tyre. A dedicated rim was made in two halves, both arranged horizontally, one half bolted to the table and the other to the punch. Airflow was controlled by a valve and when the tyre was inflated in the normal way, the two halves of the rim were pushed apart by the air pressure, giving force sufficient to drive the punch. Overall, the mechanism had been very well conceived, with guards and interlocks preventing accidental operation.

Although the entire radiotelephone industry was moving away from AM and toward FM by this time, there were still many AM channels in use together with sufficient numbers of existing customers who had need of a handheld. The decision was taken to proceed with the design of an AM handheld, to be designated T307. This presented challenges in both the receiver and transmitter. Colin McKenzie was free of his previous aviation set development and was assigned to the transmitter. I don't ever remember a time when the engineering lab had design engineers to spare and by 1981/82, John was absorbed by all the duties that accompanied his management position. The task of receiver design fell to me. I had built a 10 valve communication receiver as a schoolboy home constructor and had taken care of the finishing touches on the T302, including optimising the receiver frontend. Although I didn't find the new prospect unduly daunting, I was in awe of the vast wealth of expertise surrounding me. But my impression then, is to understate the situation. Possibly more important was the complementary nature of the skill sets. There was everyone from the graduate theorist able to visualise ideas in the real world, to the self-taught having a broad technical background. The importance of self-taught knowledge should not be underestimated. To give just two examples, universities did not teach techniques for how to make a transmitter stable or how to make a VCO (voltage controlled oscillator) impervious to chassis vibration. Very much had to be learned along the way. It can be said that the music student, while being taught the piano for example, is also absorbing the teaching method. But for the self-taught, there may or may not be a gift for teaching. Among the experienced staff, new knowledge would propagate very quickly with any confusion being cleared up in a short conversation. As a beginner in VHF RF design and when stuck on a problem, I would walk around the lab and ask several people in turn. I never had any doubt that all would have the answer. But often, one of the answers would be presented at a level within my as then limited understanding, allowing me to build knowledge.

While it may have been possible to shoehorn the T152 receiver into the handheld, its current consumption would have been too high for the limited capacity battery pack. A fresh approach was needed, beginning with the IF strip, or intermediate frequency amplifier. No suitable integrated circuits were available but there was room for four transistors. The limited distance between input and output would invite unwanted recirculation unless preventative steps were taken. Conventional IF strips presented about a volt of signal to a diode detector. By incorporating the diode into what is known as an "active circuit" the signal required from the IF strip was reduced. This in turn allowed the gain, or amplification, required of the IF strip to be reduced, taking away the risk of recirculation. Dennis Chapman was forever a fountain of novel ideas. He sometimes walked passed my bench, but on one particular occasion, he stopped and drew for me a circuit for a stacked pair of transistors. To radio frequencies, they were cascaded, with the signal passing from the output of one to the input of the other. But for DC, the current in the top transistor flowed in the bottom transistor. The result doubled the available amplification from a

A prototype T307 receiver. The added on components were part of the design process and would be incorporated into the next printed circuit board design.

given current, important in a battery powered radio. I adopted this idea with enthusiasm, two such pairs forming the IF strip. In the first amplifier of the frontend, the RF amp or radio frequency amplifier stage, current was saved by changing from a tried and true dual-gate MOSFET to a bipolar transistor. This was made possible by the availability of a transistor having a suitably low "noise figure", a measure how much unwanted additional noise an amplifier adds to the noise already present in a weak and distant signal.

No discussion about the engineering lab at Manchester St would be complete without mention of the mute, or squelch function, the latter being the term in the USA. During times of no transmission, receivers inherently produce an incessant and annoying hiss. The purpose of the "mute" is to block the receiver's audio path at all times except when receiving transmissions, even very weak ones. A knob on the front panel labelled "mute" allowed the user to set the threshold at which weak signals could open the audio path. Circuit techniques of mutes for AM and mutes for FM were different, Dennis Chapman being authoritative on the latter. Den would often come into work talking about his next "beaut new mute", or was it "new beaut mute" idea. At this same time there was always rivalry between Holden and Ford utility vehicles. One day a big ad appeared in the newspaper. "The Beaut New Ute from the General [Motors]". In no time at all someone had doctored it to relate to Den's mute and placed it on the noticeboard. In another message of endearment, someone sketched a bearded face and pinned it on the noticeboard with a mute knob placed between the lips. The mute had attracted attention not because of the personalities, but because its circuitry was hard to perfect. One of the difficulties was in discriminating between a real signal and the noise produced by an unsuppressed electrical appliance. In AM receivers a circuit to detect this noise was used to override the main signal detection voltage level from the receiver's "AGC system". One necessity in an AM receiver is a function known as AGC, automatic gain control or sometimes AVC, automatic volume control. The latter term is a little more self-

A prototype T307 transmitter circuitboard as designed by Colin McKenzie. The absence of add-on modifications speak of Colin's right first time abilities.

explanatory. The AVC or AGC function results in weak signals being automatically amplified to the same sound volume level as nearby signals. It had been a feature of valve radios since the 1930s and to this day, every AM receiver incorporates the same. In a radiotelephone, in addition to the usual functions, the AGC was required to cope with transmissions suddenly appearing and then disappearing. The correct operation of the AGC and mute represented the final two pieces of the T307 receiver to fall into place. All the while, the T307 transmitter progressed on an adjacent bench.

Colin McKenzie began as a radio operator in the merchant navy. He once told me how he had listened to the repetitive beeps from the Soviet Sputnik, the very first artificial satellite to orbit the earth, on his shortwave receiver. A dozen years later, I had been 14 years old when the first two men walked on the moon and saw this achievement as humankind's greatest endeavour. To learn that I was seated beside someone who had personally witnessed the first step of man's journey into space left me deeply in awe. I have experienced this feeling only once since, about 15 years later when I worked for Dennis Chapman's company, Swichtec. Two specialists from the USA, Rudy Severns and Ed Bloom gave seminars on power electronics in Christchurch and among the course material, included interesting tidbits from their times with the US space program in its earliest days. During a social occasion I asked Ed if he had any power supply designs on the moon. "Nothing on the moon" he said… "But I have a couple on Mars" he added. I was speechless. Since the time of Sputnik, Colin's career had moved more and more towards the technical side of radio. By the time I got to know him in the early 80s, he was a radiotelephone person extraordinaire. He had designed the transmitter in the T182c, had considerable input into sets for the aviation band and pioneered the use of variable capacitance diodes in receiver frontends within the company. The T307 transmitter was the kind of project that Colin relished, the modulator in particular presenting an interesting challenge. Modulator circuits had shrunk when converted from valve to

NEW ZEALAND POST OFFICE

TYPE APPROVAL CERTIFICATE

This is to certify that the portable radiotelephone equipment described below has been tested and found to comply with the requirements of New Zealand Post Office Specification RTA 21.

Description:	Tait T307/094108C600
Manufacturer:	Tait Electronics Ltd
Serial Number of Equipment Tested:	252084
Number of Channels:	6
Frequency Range:	94 to 108 MHz
Switching Range:	4 MHz
Power Source:	12.5 volts nominal, T306/500 mAh Nicad battery pack charged from T304/2 charger.
Remarks:	This equipment may be operated with the T253/6 Lapel Speaker-Microphone.

This certificate also applies to replicas of the set tested and to sets which have Post Office authorised modifications and this certificate remains valid only as long as all such sets meet the requirements of Specification RTA 21.

The serial number of the equipment, the name, the type of unit, the manufacturer's name, as well as any other information required to identify the equipment shall be indelibly marked on the unit in a conspicuous and/or readily accessible location, and in a manner to ensure its permanency during the expected lifetime of the equipment in its normal environment.

Any proposed changes to the above equipment should be notified to the Post Office as unauthorised modifications will invalidate this certificate.

RBVernall

(R. B. VERNALL)
for Director-General.
19.9.83

A T307 Type Approval Certificate

transistor for the hybrid sets. They shrunk again for the T152. Another shrink would be required for the T307. This was made possible by the availability of an audio power amplifier integrated circuit that Philips had produced for use in car radios. The component was thin, such that it could be placed at the edge of the circuitboard in proximity with the chassis, which would absorb the unwanted heat from it. The use of this integrated circuit reduced the amount of copper wire needed in the modulation transformer, in turn, reducing the bulk of this component. It was these innovations that made a VHF AM handheld a possibility. But in addition to just being possible, the T307 complied with the same exacting standards as the mobile product. At this time in New Zealand the Post Office set these standards as they were responsible for all communication, not just post, telegraph and telephone. Compliance with the standard was known as Type Approval.

Formal type testing was carried out at independent test laboratories. Before submitting a product, identical tests were carried out in-house. The test benches and personnel for this were situated in the southeast corner of the engineering lab at Manchester Street. In addition to testing at the end of development, various tests were often carried out along the way for reassurance that the design was within spec and also to discover any non-compliances as soon as possible. In a tribute to this, someone had scratched with chalk on an old piece of blackboard:

Exceeds spec: talks to God

Meets spec: talks to Angus

Almost meets spec: talks to self

Below spec: Argues with self

Well below spec: loses arguments with self

For the T307, tests went largely as expected except that occasionally a modulator integrated circuit would fail, with reason for the failure elusive.

From the very beginning, Colin had needed to know whether the car audio integrated circuits would be suitable in the intended application and had tested them under very harsh conditions just to be sure. Now they appeared to be failing under very mild conditions and the situation was beginning to concern onlookers. Although strictly not my place to do so, I went to see the testing technician and fortunately he was very forthcoming with information, mentioning that it had failed when he changed its supply voltage. During testing it had been normal procedure that many tests would be conducted at three voltages, low, nominal and high. The voltage was provided by a bench power supply and rather than tediously adjusting the voltage using the supply's adjustment knob each time, the technician had modified the power supply by fitting it with a low-nominal-high selector switch. The penny immediately dropped. As the selector switch was moved from one position to the next, the voltage was spiking high, causing instant damage to the modulator integrated circuit. When the wiring of the selector switch in the faulty power supply was corrected, there were no more failures. The modulator turned out to be so effective and so reliable that an uprated version of it was used in the future T510 AM mobile set.

In the middle of this project somewhere, John brought to work a poster about project progression.

Phases of a Project

Exaltation

Confusion

Disenchantment

Search for the Guilty

Punishment of the Innocent

Distinction to the Uninvolved

Colin, John and I mused that if we could keep a project in the upper confusion region, we'd be doing OK. Someone joked that an absence of confusion would imply that the project was not ambitious enough. Near the end, a management decision dictated that the handheld range should include a version of the T307 suitable for use on the aviation band. Colin went to work immediately and designed the modifications for both the receiver and transmitter. The aviation requirement included a production request for fifteen additional prototypes and although this did delay the entry into service, the design had progressed to schedule.

The Money

When arriving at Christchurch Branch late 1976 or early 1977 from memory, I remember saying to someone that I still did not know what Angus Tait looked like. This, together with other memories, places a Manchester Street company meeting in mid 1977. All staff from all departments were invited. The meeting was called so that Angus could announce a milestone. A one million dollar turnover for the very first time, with a tenth of this coming from export sales. Angus went on to say he could foresee a time when export sales would become ten times domestic sales. Many sources talk of the success of export sales in the years that followed. The Muldoon government offered export incentives. In what must have been 1981 or 1982 a rumour circulated claiming that the export incentives had changed the books from loss to profit. The numbers, if my memory serves me well, were staggering. A loss of almost $300k before tax translated to a profit of near a million dollars after tax, where the "tax" included the export incentives. Around that same time in the early 1980s there had been a hiccup with sales to South Africa. There are always exemptions to sanctions so that emergency services, utility companies and the like don't lose efficiency. To avoid any confusion, a shipment was sent under a different brand name. Tait labels were removed from chassis and replaced with the new name. New front panels were printed with the new name. The "T" in the centre of each microphone was removed and replaced with the new logo. Except that in at least one case, the "T" was not removed before the new logo was affixed. Unfortunately a "T" was discovered hiding below the new label and the situation quickly made the headlines here. However, I don't remember any repercussions and so presume the sale to have been compliant with the sanctions.

Around this same time, and before the move to Wairakei Road, Angus took on a general manager. The idea was that with a general manager at the helm, Angus himself would be free to look to the bigger picture. The new manager, Graeme Stairmand had been a colleague of my retired neighbour at Andersons, the Christchurch engineering and boilermaker company. Unfortunately, things didn't work out. My neighbour came over to ask what had gone wrong. I knew only that the departure had been very sudden and told my neighbour so. My neighbour explained how that was always the way in corporate circles. Angus returned to the helm, but not before initiating one-on-one interviews with all his engineering staff. I felt very privileged to be included here. But Angus' sincere endeavour had unfortunate repercussions. Inflation was eroding real wages. Professional consulting engineers were always well rewarded. Government engineers, as for all government employees, traditionally had salaries commensurate with their good working conditions, good superannuation schemes and good job security. IE, salaries were always less than in the private sector. In 1974 a government Higher Salaries Commission got the power to set remuneration for MPs based on salaries in the private sector. The PSA, public service association or union for public sector employees, managed to cling to the coat tails of the Higher Salaries Commission and boost all public service pay to levels approaching the highest in the private sector while also retaining all the other benefits listed above. This left the engineers at Tait at the bottom of the heap. A salary survey in a NZ engineering magazine proved it so.

When a dozen "experts" in almost as many central banks worldwide held interest rates too low for too long post Covid-19 and reignited inflation, they cannot have remembered the pain of the 70s and 80s. These were tough times. Any annual pay rise less than annual inflation amounted to a pay cut. To add insult to injury, the government did not increase tax thresholds with inflation. This meant that even when an annual pay rise matched inflation, proportionately more would attract higher tax and reduce effective take home pay. All income earners in the country, all the way up and down the pay scales felt the pain. And so when the survey page was placed on your desk with a finger pointing to a salary, it became impossible to deny that Tait engineers were at the bottom of the heap. Looking back, I see the tragedy for Angus. He had been sincere in his quest to find the aspirations of his engineers only to have his efforts stir up a hornets' nest of discontent. We all knew that Angus did not live a lavish lifestyle himself. (In a totally unrelated meeting about building-security, a manager warned us that Angus had had his wallet stolen from his downstairs office. A voice in the audience quipped: it was welded shut!) I once went to his residence with Chris Chao to borrow his Land Rover for a Field Engineering trip to the Mt Grey repeater site. The abode was neat, tidy and humble. An uprising always has ringleaders. I don't think any staff simply followed these ringleaders like sheep hoping for greener pastures. I myself felt aggrieved, an aggrievement made worse by the survey. So when the management called a staff meeting to address the issue, I was there with everyone else. An early speaker was Peter Cornes, a bearded, pipe smoking personnel manager who occupied one of the lonely offices off the Manchester St foyer. I remember him discharging his duties well and as an original thinker who deservedly held the full confidence and trust of Angus. In an unrelated comment at a different time, he was able to dismiss the popular view that "airline pilots were just glorified bus drivers" with an example. "Walk along a plank spanning two chairs." he had said. "Now walk the same plank spanning two skyscrapers." He then explained how the two jobs were identical, but the consequences of error were vastly different. When Peter Cornes spoke at the meeting, he did not talk wage rises. He reversed the perspective and spoke for his audience: If you go to buy an appliance, you don't go and buy the most expensive, you shop around to find the best value for money. "So why should an employer pay the most extravagant wages?" he asked. It was an unpalatable view, but one that an engineer's mind could not deny. I don't remember how Angus began, only what happened when one of the ringleaders interjected. What Angus then delivered would have impressed even Aristotle, who had said of anger, "*Anybody can become angry - that is easy, but to be angry with the right person and to the right degree and at the right time and for the right purpose and in the right way - that is not within everybody's power and is not easy.*" Following the interjection, Angus' reaction mirrored Aristotle's teaching. Not brief, but clear, quickly spoken and devastating. When finished, you could have heard a track-pin drop.

In the days that followed, the rebellion faded. I don't remember it resulting in significant changes to pay scales. Some cynically muttered that the ringleaders had been paid off. But I think the truth was much simpler. We all had the best jobs in the world. For sure the absolute leading edge of radio communication belonged to the US military and NASA. But for VHF and UHF point to point communication for the commercial sector, Tait had surpassed Motorola in many areas. Working creatively at this level provided good job satisfaction and this compensated for the relatively poor pay. Another compensation was the superannuation scheme.

The Tait superannuation scheme should have been good. It was a lump sum scheme set for retirement at 60. The employee contribution was 5% from each pay packet. This was matched by the employer contribution. After 10 years, the employer contribution doubled to 10%. Before government meddling somewhere along the way, the contributions had been from pretax wages. The scheme had everything going for it. But like everything else in the 70s and 80s, inflation eroded it. In the late 80s a long serving employee retired from head office after having been in the scheme for about twenty years. His lump sum was similar to one annual salary. His contributions of 5% each year for twenty years tallied to one annual salary. In other words, he recovered his contribution, but not the company's contribution. In fact, very few investments in those years could head off inflation. One feature of the Tait scheme was that when an employee left the company, his or her account was cashed up and paid out. The decision to change jobs is never an easy one. There are always many things to consider and the superannuation payout became one more reason for leaving. The sad irony is of course that the scheme that Angus put in place for the welfare of this staff became a motive for them to leave. Not that Angus would try to keep his staff unwillingly. My impression was that he liked having long serving staff but not to the point of keeping prisoners. Burt Van Dissel, one of the “last eight” (page viii) and "first twelve" and working at Christchurch Branch in the mid-70s, spoke of an earlier conversation he’d had with Angus regarding his future. Angus had said, “…you’re always a free agent.” meaning that Angus would hold no hard feelings if Burt found greener pastures. Additionally, I don’t remember any bad blood when Charles Dickey, John Croft and Colin McKenzie moved to their own company, Salcom.

Documentation

It may be said that while some mechanical engineers might choose to design weapons systems, all civil engineers design targets. In the early days at Tait Electronics, the mechanical designers were not graduate engineers but very skilled practitioners from the trades, often having advanced theoretical qualifications. The original mechanical person, John Rowe, features in both the "last 8" and "first 12" photographs (page viii). John Croft, also in both these photos, told me some related stories. There is a kind of screw that has a hexagonal hole in the head instead of the more usual screwdriver slot or Phillips cross. These were known an Allen screws but were more often just referred to as hexagon screws. The Tait manufacturing people had suggested that a particular screw be changed to a hexagon type to help solve an assembly problem. When the written request reached John Rowe, a typo had changed hexagon to mexagon. So John immediately took to his lathe and turned up a screw with a large head in the shape of a sombrero and presented this to the manufacturing staff! Another intriguing tale related to John Rowe's apprentice "training". He would have the drill press at the ready, with drill bit fitted. He would give the apprentice a thin steel plate to be drilled, with all the drilling points centre punched. Drill presses invariably had a reverse-off-forward switch on the right hand side, being the same side as the drill's up-down lever. John Rowe would demonstrate the first hole while the apprentice watched from the left and then switch off. "Now you try", John would say as he left the room. Returning after a minute, John would feign surprise at the lack of progress as the apprentice hauled as hard as he could on the down lever. "Let me try", John would offer… straight through! John had cunningly sharpened his prank drill bit backwards. For the demo, with observer out of sight of the switch, John would switch the drill into reverse whereupon the reverse-sharpened drill bit would willingly cut. I never did hear how this ended, the apprentice being told and seeing the funny side or still puzzled at knockoff time.

At Manchester St, the mechanical workshop associated with the lab was well equipped with guillotine, folder, milling machine and fly-press together with all the usual workshop tools. Fly-presses generally had a cast iron ball fitted over the handle to add inertia, and the ball from this one was occasionally borrowed for the end of the chain when required at a stag party. Mechanical engineers had their own drawing boards, because part of their craft involved the ability to translate the three dimensional structures in their heads down onto two dimensional paper. In 1981, the mechanical engineer count was three, Lisle Hood in the handheld group, Howard Pegram in the basestation group and Peter May in the mobile group. It was around this time that the T490 synthesised sets were in development. The core of a synthesiser is a circuit known as a Voltage Controlled Oscillator or VCO. Such circuits are very sensitive to external electromagnetic fields and the simplest way to protect them is with shielding. Peter May designed a deep drawn cover for this purpose. He then designed and built a pressing tool so that he could make a small number, as confirmation of a satisfactory design. The next step was for the supplier to independently make their own tool which would go on to make the production volumes needed. However, the supplier could not get their tool to work properly and so Peter asked for it to be delivered to his Tait workshop where he soon found the centring to be off. He immediately went for the expedient solution of repositioning the alignment pins himself. After testing it to confirm correct operation he sent it back to a happy supplier, any not directly involved being none the wiser. Also around this time there were some staff changes. Howard accepted a management position at Betacom, one of Christchurch's largest suppliers of metalwork and from memory, was replaced by Paul Fewings. Lisle opted for self-employment, a sign in a Ferry Road hedge marking his design office for a great many years into the future. Steve Allen arrived with a diploma in industrial design and took up the mechanical position in the handheld group. By this time the existing handheld, basestation and mobile designs were nearing completion and a new mobile product was being anticipated that would need the combined efforts of all the mechanical designers. Accordingly, the group "rebranded" and applied some stylish interior design touches to their abode.

Mechanical designers could generally do the whole job from concept to drawings, whereas electronics designers could not. Drawing office personnel were required to prepare schematic diagrams to standards of clarity and neatness that were beyond the average electronic designer. Wayne Worrall was the master craftsman here. All drafting personnel used a drawing board and stencils for lines and the various symbols. For text, some preferred to use stencils while others opted for freehand. In Wayne's drawings, the text was freehand and very neat, quickly written and easy to read, but with a nice characteristic style. All drawings, mechanical or electrical, were made on a semi clear sheet material with a frosted finish, A1 and A2 being the most used sizes. Actual sized prints were made on an ammonia printer, the faint smell sometimes gently wafting through the lab.

The one thing that most electronic engineers did prefer to do themselves was the printed circuit board artwork. Although the resulting printed circuit boards usually looked highly technically advanced, the twice full sized artworks that they were made from were composed using crude methods. Narrow self-adhesive tapes from Bishop Graphics were stuck down onto transparent Mylar sheet. Where holes were to be drilled, the centre holes in self-adhesive doughnut shapes marked the spots. For components such as integrated circuits that required holes in set patterns, matching assemblages of doughnuts were available pre placed on transparent stickers. Even at twice full size, it was exacting work. In many circumstances the proximity of one component to another or even the exact length of a track could affect the performance of the design. It was for this reason that the electronic engineers usually did their own artworks but this was slowly changing by the early 80s.

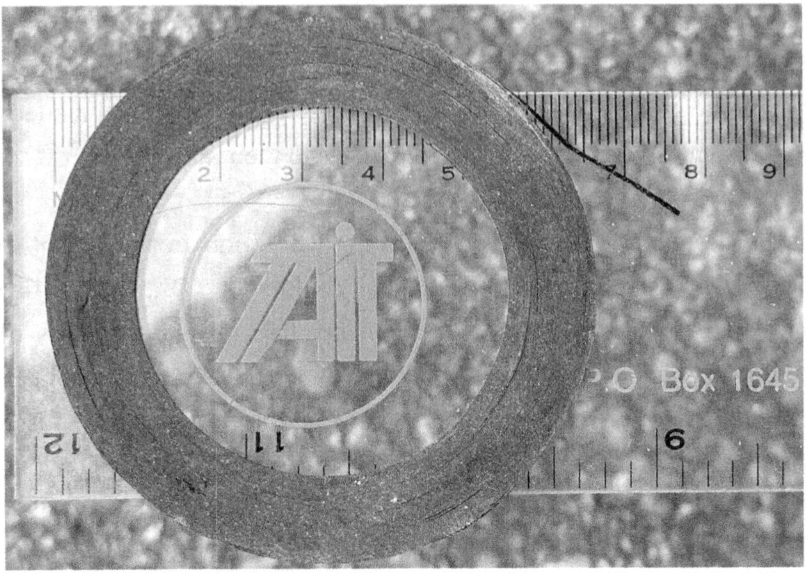

A roll of 1 millimetre wide Bishop Graphics tape on a Tait ruler.

From memory, the Tait computer system was from the American giant NCR, National Cash Register. It was well entrenched when I started in 1976 and I think I remember the pay slips looking computer printed. One of its main functions was for inventory management, including parts listing. Each component was assigned a ten digit IPN, or Internal Part Number. Fan folded printouts with lists of all components together with pricing made it easy for engineers to keep tabs on product costs as a design progressed. As a design firmed up, engineers would provide hand written information to the parts listing group who would enter the parts list into the computer system. In early 80s Manchester St, this group was made up of Peter Graham, John Anderson, Debbie Tennant and technician Paul Morrison temporarily. These people had to be very thorough because no means of automated checking were available. The final step was for the engineers involved with the design to double check the computer printout. Adjacent this group was the technical writers' office, run by a gentlemanly Bill Bird and offsider, Janice Bell. I wrote technical descriptions for the T307. I knew how these things worked but didn't know how to write. To the contrary, the technical authors knew how to write but didn't know how things worked. Perhaps they slowly beat me into shape as I later drew the short straw and had to write technical descriptions for the T500s. Manuals always included the schematic, often as a foldout, plan views of printed circuit boards and various mechanical assembly drawings. Fortunately, photographs were not necessary, as they were either poor quality or too expensive. But there were situations where a plan view alone was inadequate because some field modifications required wires to be routed or parts to be fitted in ways that defied a plan view or description. In the absence of photographs, illustrations had to be prepared and Joe Fone proved to be a natural at this work. These drawings, when printed in manuals, would photocopy clearly, whereas photographs didn't copy well at all. Joe was also proficient with Bishop Graphics tapes, and having come from a technical background, was able to do some of the artworks that engineers had previously had to do themselves. It was an example of one of the many things that made Tait Electronics Tick. That is, to recognise a skill and position it to everyone's advantage. Joe went on to do many of the artworks for the T500 series, freeing up engineers to carry on designing.

When Paul Morrison wasn't in the parts listing group, he was working alongside Greg Ewing in the basestation group. Greg was an engineering graduate from the University of Canterbury, very theoretical but also practical, having come from a North Otago farm. While at Tait, one of his home projects was a miles per gallon meter for his 1600cc Lancia, twenty years before this technology became commonplace. In March 1981, he published an in-house paper: Characterising Sources of Intermodulation in Radio Receivers. Although highly theoretical, it was presented in a way that made it accessible to mortals and I found it invaluable during my years designing receivers. Greg was an early adopter of a programmable HP calculator with a liquid crystal display. I listened intently when Paul related Greg's impressions. The only negative was that the display could be difficult to read when basking on the lawn in the sun. This incited Paul to coin the term, "recreational mathematics". Greg's skillset allowed the Tait lab to be an early adopter of the IBM PC which prepared the way for the first computer simulations of circuits within the company. All the while Greg was also focussed on circuit design, but would soon be totally wrenched away from this.

CHARACTERISING SOURCES OF INTERMODULATION IN RADIO RECEIVERS

G. Ewing 22nd March 1981

INTRODUCTION

With the increasing use of radio-communications, the radio frequency spectrum is becoming more congested. One of the consequences of this is that receivers are required to pick out their signal from an increasing array of others. Any non-linearities in the system will cause mixing of the signals, to further proliferate the spectral components. Intermodulation is caused by a particular type of non-linearity.

Intermodulation has particular significance for any radio system where channel spacing is constant, which is very often the case. This is because intermodulation products fall exactly on adjacent channels in such a system. Once generated, the IM (intermodulation) signal is on channel, so it is not possible to filter it out.

Therefore we must aim at minimising IM in all parts of the system. The techniques shown in this paper describe characterising radio receivers, but are equally applicable to any parts of a system which cause IM.

The abstract/introduction of Greg's paper on intermodulation.

After the move to Wairakei Rd, the company invested in CAD, or Computer Aided Design, opting for an IBM mainframe and several terminals. Their flatscreen, cathode ray tube colour displays were absolute leading edge, having a resolution that would not be seen on personal computers for another decade. Greg managed the entire project all the way through selection, purchase and ongoing use. It was a very large spend for the company with total cost said to be around the million dollars. Although expensive, the IBM purchase included installation, setup and training. It ran two CAD systems, CATIA for mechanical design and CBDS for printed circuit board design. At first glance, it might have appeared to be counterproductive for the design of printed circuit boards. For the existing method, the drawing office would be preparing the schematic at the same time that the engineer was working on the artwork. For the CAD approach, the schematic had to be completed before the design of the printed circuit board artwork could begin. Where new components were used for the very first time within the company, they usually had to be entered into the CAD system before work on the schematic could begin. This made it appear that the million dollar CAD process might be slower than the manual process. It was necessary to look at the bigger picture to see past this. Drawing the schematic in CAD was doing much more than merely drawing a picture. It allowed the parts list to be created automatically. It generated connectivity details that simplified the design process for the printed circuit board which meant that skilled layout technicians could do more of what engineers had traditionally done, Joe Fone being an instant starter. These features were impressive, but the real game changer was the output. Rather than artworks that could stretch, crease or have Bishop Graphics tapes peeled off by carelessness, all outputs were in digital format and drove the printed circuit board manufacturers' numerically controlled equipment directly, speeding up board delivery times.

The mechanical package, CATIA, was from the French aerospace company Dassault, known for its Falcon business jet and Mirage fighter. Just as for CBDS, advantages didn't become obvious until looking at the big picture. Building the three dimensional models in the system was a highly skilled and laborious task. But once done, the product could be seen from any aspect and the fit of any part to any other easily analysed. Just as for printed circuit boards, the digital file formats from CATIA could drive the metalwork suppliers' numerically controlled equipment directly, thereby shortening lead times. The T500 was done the old fashioned way but an externally identical series ii version of this known as the T505 series, was designed on the new CAD system. I remember coming back to work after a year at university and seeing the results for the very first time. I remember observing the registration between printed circuit board mounting holes and the corresponding screw threads on the heatsink to which it would attach. The alignment was absolute perfection.

The CAD system took the company a big jump forward in a short space of time but did highlight some building issues along the way. The circular saw shape of the building's roof had obviously presented some challenges to its builders. Put simply, it leaked. One issue was that expansion and contraction of the long sheets of material turned nail holes into nail slots. Placing expensive workstations under this roof came with some risk but a simple and effective solution was devised. A cover of corrugated plastic roofing material was erected above the area containing work stations. The IBM mainframe and associated equipment was housed in its own room under a mezzanine floor near the central core of the building. The building's heating and ventilation system, housed in the basement, was based on heat pump technology that offered heating and cooling functions. Rather than anticipating today's practice of using outside air as the heat reservoir, it used artesian water. Water from aquifers was pumped up and through a heat exchanger and then returned. Fresh air intake was via a basement level tunnel to the building's periphery which doubled as direct access to the rear carpark. In spite of its sophistication, the system struggled to keep the building cool during hot norwesters. While the staff sweltered, the air-cooled IBM CAD mainframe system was surrounded by pleasant cool air from its room's own dedicated aircon. The CAD system was very reliable and was used to the max, soon requiring two shifts with work beginning at 6AM for the morning crew. With more intensive use came the need for an upgrade. The original IBM mainframe was replaced by a competing NAS (National Advanced Systems) unit that Greg had found second hand and on which the IBM software would run. Greg also managed to find half a dozen compatible hard drive units. Each was the size of a washing machine and had a capacity of 40MB. Today, thirty five years later, a cell phone has a thousand times that storage.

After the move to Wairakei Rd, the engineering head count steadily grew. People came and went, too many to remember in fact. By the late 80s, Dave Reynolds was the lead technical writer, using a Xerox word processor. The large portrait oriented black and white display could present an A4 page actual size and exactly as it would later come from the printer. The system stored documents on 8-inch floppy discs. Steve Allen led the T500 series mechanical design through to completion and then departed and successfully established his own industrial design business. As mentioned elsewhere, Dennis Chapman had established Eltec in the mid-80s to which Peter May defected, others following over the years, including me. In the new environment, Peter completed the mechanical design of a very attractive and practical industrial product range, all from his drawing board. Eltec changed its name to Swichtec and then introduced CAD mid-90s when the technology was both more mature and more affordable. Peter is still doing CAD design work to this day for a range of clients. Paul Fewings joined Swichtec from where he went on to excel in building services management. Ian Crawley had arrived early to mid-80s with a diploma in industrial design from memory. He put this to good use in the design of the T2000, a product completely designed on CAD, Ian being a natural at the workstation. In the 90s he departed and established his own design consultancy. Dave Mason was another whose mechanical expertise went into the design of the T2000. Outside of work he could extract quiet jazz from unusual combinations of keys at the piano.

Any discussion of documentation in this era would be incomplete without mention of the photocopier, the most taken for granted office product of the 70 and 80s. Firstly, it was the TikTok of the time. Someone would bring a cartoon picture, or meme, to work and photocopy it. Copies would go out-tray to in-tray or sometimes be put on a noticeboard if savoury. People would then make their own copies, take them home and give them to others who would repeat the process at their places of work. It was the "viral" of the age. The same pictures did the rounds again via the fax of the 80s and yet one more time via email in the 90s. But more than anything else, the photocopier promoted the concept of parallel design, the idea that various people can execute various parts of a design at the same time, rather than one after the other. It is such an obvious idea that one has to wonder why even write about it. But now take the photocopier away. The idea is still obvious but the means getting the necessary upfront information to each player has vanished. As an example, an engineer hand draws a schematic, rubbings out and corrections making carbon paper highly impractical. Four photocopies are made. 1, order-in-advance components circled red, sent to purchasing. 2, master for schematic, sent to drawing office. 3, master for parts list, given to technician. 4, master for printed circuit board artwork, keeps for self. Without the photocopier, 2 would have to happen first, followed by 1, 3 and 4 getting ammonia prints. By the late 80s, PCs were being used for the writing and printing of reports, Tony Berggren always having good knowledge of the best application software and utility programs. Those of us that were slow at the keyboard were able to give the handwritten draft to reception, have it typed into Borland Sprint and returned on a 5 inch floppy disc so that we could do the final editing ourselves. The dot matrix printers had a mode, NLQ meaning "Near Letter Quality", but the output still did not look as

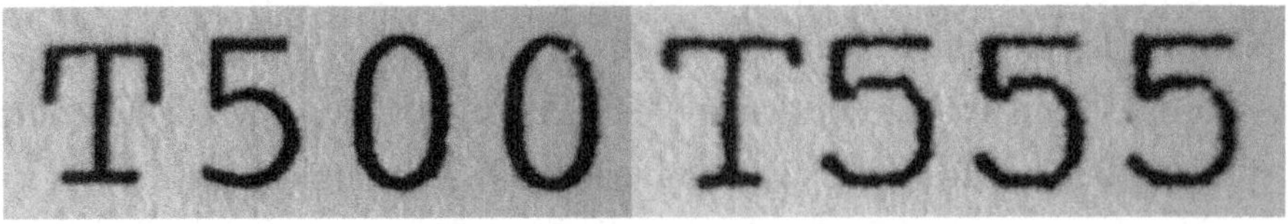

Magnification of titles of T500 reports printed late-80s. Type writer at left, NLQ from dot matrix printer at right. For an example of draft quality from a dot matrix printer, see the power bill in the first chapter.

good as from a type writer. Where illustrations were required, gaps were left in the text and images glued onto the printed pages. These pages were then photocopied to "print" the original report.

If there was ever a "most important" document, it was the type approval certificate. In New Zealand, the Post Office had published the standards to which radiotelephones had to comply. Type Approval testing was a serious endeavour which had to be conducted by an independent test laboratory, usually in Australia. To be certain of passing this, all tests were replicated in house by Tait's own type approval department, run by Lester Parkes. Lester was a university graduate of similar vintage to Greg and essentially had two jobs wrapped onto one. Lester would read and interpret the type approval standards so that he could assist engineers in understanding their requirements as well as organise his testing technicians. There was no let up because for every new market that Tait wanted to venture into, its type approval requirements would have to be assessed. In addition to the radio aspects, all power supply and battery charging equipment had to meet electrical safety standards. An interesting set of circumstances surrounded the testing of the battery charger for the handhelds in the early 80s. The unit passed the official testing but was returned with a burnt out mains transformer. To test the unit's fuse, a short circuit was applied to the output of the transformer. But somehow, someone at Taits had fitted a five or ten Amp fuse instead of the correct quarter Amp fuse and when it was tested, the fuse didn't blow but instead, the transformer burnt out. Because the unit didn't get dangerously hot or catch fire, it still passed the test. As if to add insult to injury, a sentence within the test report contained words to the effect: Your battery charger doesn't actually need a fuse, but because it was there we had to test it.

Competitor Products

During my time at Christchurch Branch in 1977 and 1978, there were still customers operating both the Tait Century Series and the competing Pye Cambridge. Pye were an English company who had acquired Akrad (Auckland Radio) in the years following the war and who had a very large manufacturing facility in the Coromandel town of Waihi. They were large producers of radios and television sets in addition to modest numbers of radiotelephones. As explained in the chapter "Moorhouse Ave", Norm, the workshop foreman believed the Cambridge to be a better product than the Century Series. After the Tait T152 was released in New Zealand, Pye responded with their all transistor Galaxy. It was large and flimsy and inferior to the T152 in every way. Of the Pye Galaxy, Norm could only say, "Something went wrong." As Pye customers became Tait customers, many staff from the Pye radiotelephone outlets took up jobs in Tait Sales and Service.

It is not unusual for manufacturers to study competitor product. For Tait, copying was never the motive. The Tait engineering personnel always had the ambition to make better product than the competition, never the same as. One example was transmitter current consumption. Competitor sets from the USA tended to draw 10 to 20% more transmitter current than Tait sets having identical power output. There was some irony here because the power transistors used in the Tait sets were often of US manufacture. The datasheets for these specialist semiconductors usually included application information that gave engineers a head start in their adoption. This begs the question: Given that all had the same head start, why did Tait product have the lower current consumption?

During transmitter development work, the RF (radio frequency) output that flows out from its transmission-line is not connected to an antenna, but instead, to what is referred to as a "dummy load". That is, a resistor designed for high frequency operation that simply turns the transmitted power into heat. The reasons for this are twofold. Firstly it prevents any unwanted transmission from the design lab. Secondly, the dummy load behaves as if it is an ideal antenna. A transistor supplier's application information is all based on performance into a dummy load. If every antenna was perfectly designed, perfectly installed, perfectly tuned and perfectly maintained, then simply duplicating the transistor manufacturer's application circuit would be the end of the job. But the reality of an antenna is different. From a poorly setup antenna, some of the power reaching it will be reflected back along the transmission-line, being returned to the transmitter's output transistor. From a badly damaged antenna, almost all of the power may be reflected back. Rarely, the reflected power could cause damage, but as time went on, transmitting transistors were ruggedised against this. The major issue stemming from a defective antenna was transmitter instability. The transmitter, instead of behaving as an amplifier as intended, could behave as an oscillator and generate interfering signals across the spectrum. This highly undesirable situation had to be guarded against when a transmitter was designed. It was the hardest aspect of transmitter design. It was beyond any computer simulation available to Tait. There was always a trade-off between stability and current consumption. A job well done required much trial and error and much dedication, but the rewards were rich: Stable transmitters that drew less current than their competitors.

Throughout the 1970s, Tait Electronics set up comprehensive networks of overseas sales offices from where staff were able to get a good reach into many markets. In addition to drumming up sales, sometimes information on competitor product would be found. In the mid-1980s, a competitor product from Asia was brought into the engineering lab at Wairakei Rd where it provided much interest and amusement to the engineering staff.

Whoever found it also got hold of its service manual, complete with circuit diagram. Much of the circuitry was a direct copy of the Tait T530, the VHF FM version of the T500 series. The only major deviation was in the transmitter. Whereas the T500 was entirely built on a single circuitboard, the copy had followed the Asian practice of devoting an individual board to the transmitter power stages. For Tait engineers involved with any new and original design, it was not unusual to see potential for very minor

A 1980s tie pin. Blue enamel on gold.

improvement only after approaching production deadlines had closed the door on any changes. As a harsh self-judgment, these lost opportunities were often seen as mistakes. As the T530 designers were poring over the Asian schematic, one noticed the same lost opportunities and said, "Look, they've even copied our mistakes!" Another quoted an old saying: Plagiarism is the sincerest form of flattery.

The flattery continued. From the days of AM Tait Limited, the company had provided mains power supplies to allow the mobile radiotelephones to be used in offices. For the T152 and later AM sets, there was a compact AC power supply that included a loudspeaker at front and Red Range connector at rear that the radiotelephone plugged into. The combination of power supply and radiotelephone, about the size of a shoebox, was a neat looking office product in the day.

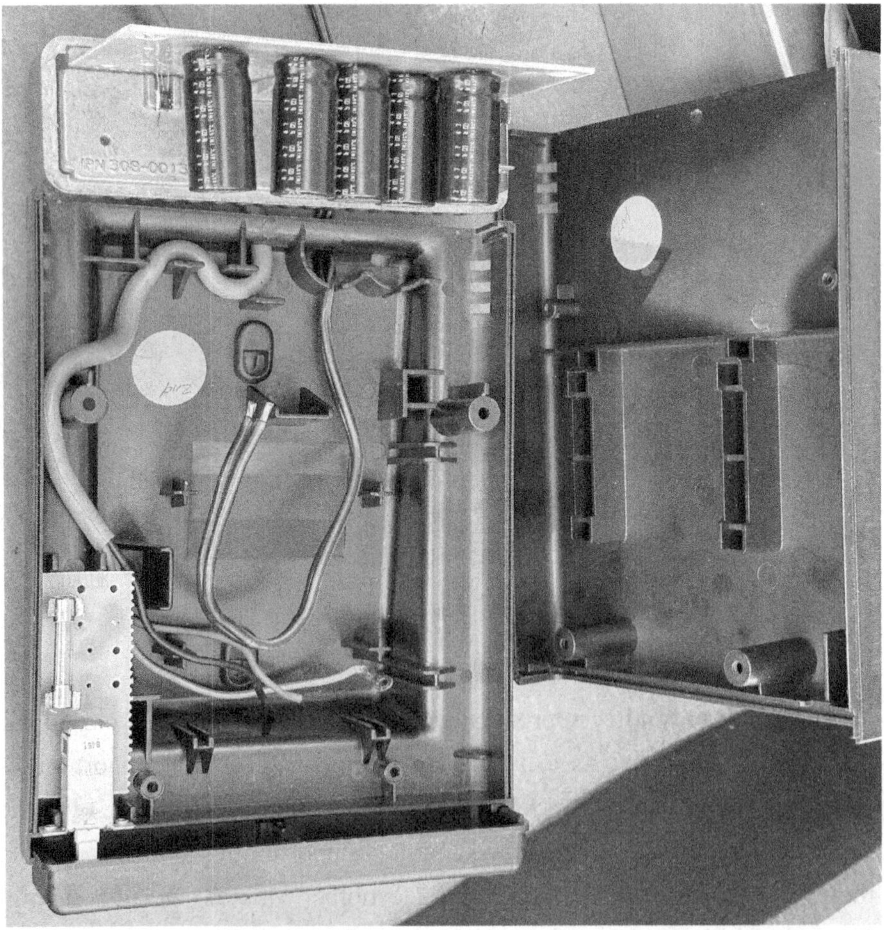

Enclosure pieces for the T500 Power Supply, the T508.

Power supplies needed what is known as a "regulating function", so that the output remained at a steady 12 Volts regardless of actual AC mains voltage or required current delivery. This necessary regulating function came at the expense of wasted heat. The later T500 series had a power supply specifically designed for it too. As Tait expertise in the field increased, so too did the efficiency of the power supplies. The T500 power supply, while still employing a conventional mains transformer, incorporated what is known as "switchmode" technology to provide the regulating function with less wasted heat. Its plastic enclosure, designed by Peter May and Ian Crawley, incorporated some interesting features. Resilient mounting of the heavy mains transformer allowed for a fall from a desk without breakage. Cable restraints were integrated. Initially there had been some concern that the abrupt entry point for the mains cable might result in fraying and eventual cracking of copper strands over a lifetime of cable flexing. To remove any doubt, Peter simply rigged the cable onto a windshield wiper mechanism and left it overnight to endure many lifetimes of flexing without failure.

As well as power supplies for mobile units in offices, Tait were making power supplies for their extensive range of repeater or basestation equipment. In the 1990s, the products fully embraced switchmode technology, resulting in compact sized units producing little wasted heat. When I moved to Swichtec Power Systems at the beginning of 1991, I had had no prior involvement with the switchmode units being developed at Tait. Then in the late 1990s, an engineer from Tait paid us a visit with half a dozen switchmode power supplies under his arm. They were all plug-in units having a front panel about 200mm high by 50mm wide and all measured approximately 300mm front to back. All had had their covers removed to allow inspection. The engineer placed the 5 or 6 units side by side on a table and drew attention to their internal similarities. Only one was a Tait product. Of the copies, one was almost identical, the others displaying varying degrees of originality. As mentioned in other chapters, engineering staff at Tait Electronics found tremendous job satisfaction in the creativity and originality of their work. I don't remember any engineers who would have bothered getting up in the morning for a day's work of copying. Apparently, that can't have been a problem elsewhere in the world.

The Hundreds of the Eighties

While at Manchester St it was not unusual to hear "low cost set" or "cheapie" in the conversation followed by a description of some technology that might promote lower cost. By this time the AM sets, the T190 FM sets, the T490 synthesised sets and the handheld products were all in steady production and as their engineering support requirements diminished, engineering minds were being freed. Export markets were expanding and as production volumes grew, a concept known as "economies of scale" beckoned. The T190 sets had an extruded heatsink. The upfront costs for a purpose designed extrusion are low but the unit cost for each extruded heatsink is high due to all the post processing such as cutting and drilling. To the contrary, a diecast heatsink as being proposed for the "cheapie" would have a low unit cost but very high upfront, or tooling cost. The same reasoning applied to using injection moulded plastic parts for the enclosure as opposed to sheet metal. For the high production volumes expected for the "low cost set", the high upfront tooling costs were expected to add very little to each unit. This was all happening in the later days at Manchester St. A few years prior, the components store had moved to the ground floor area beyond the foyer, and the first floor cafeteria had expanded into the area vacated by the store meaning that there was now room for some of the smaller staff functions. There were many faces at Manchester Street by this time but the proximity of the various departments made it easier to see who was who compared to the times when the departments had been scattered. One young woman from head office would sometimes bring a late twenties sister to social events. At such events many would stand against the painted chipboard partition wall on the north side of the cafeteria, some with arms folded and others with arms at sides, including with palms against the wall. After one such social event, a fellow technician described how he'd had a bout of hiccups when standing at the wall and that the sister to one side of him suggested that a fright would cure his ailment. He said he got half way through protesting, "That doesn't work!" when her hand departed the wall and inflicted a grope. He said it cured his hiccups. The cafeteria was a little too distant from the lab for regular lunch use, most eating at desks and getting coffee in disposable cups from the click-clack dispenser within the area. I had managed to devise a budget lunch of cheese between two slices of North's Bread, similar to the Vogel's of today. I scavenged a blunt but unbroken hacksaw blade from the rubbish bin in the workshop. Every midday this would slice cheese from the block with the subsequent bread cutting also cleaning the "knife". Then one day when walking passed my bench, Joe Fone suddenly stopped, picked up the blade, dangled it vertically from between finger and thumb, sighted along it and let it go. It disappeared trough a crack between the floor boards. I never again found an unbroken blade. For the "cheapie", miniaturisation techniques, such as stand-up resistors and intensive use of integrated circuits, were borrowed from the handhelds so that the printed circuit board count could be reduced from the three in the T190s back to the one of the AM sets. These ideas set the scene for a low cost set, but the name evolved. The term "cheapie" was abandoned for fear it might evoke a suspicion of poor quality. "Low cost set" was replaced with a different euphemism, "value for money set". Once the project became official it was thereafter known as the T500 series. Initially two models were proposed, the T550 UHF set and the T530 VHF set. But soon the T510 VHF AM set was added into the mix.

Up until this time, complete radiotelephones had usually been designed by just one or two people with a third wrapping some metalwork around it near the end. Because of the long lead times for the tooling for both the diecast aluminium parts and the injection moulded parts, mechanical design had to win the toss and kick off first. Steve Allen took the helm with assistance from Gordon Todd together with the others from the mechanical design group. Steve's mission had to include the areas of the printed circuit board that interfaced with the controls and indicators at front, and with the heatsink and connectors at rear. Dennis Chapman had a lot of involvement with what would go where on the circuitboard and supervised the hands-on engineers, particularly for the synthesiser and receiver circuits. By this time, the use of the word "group" was expanding. Given UHF, VHF and AM models in the product range, it made sense to have as much commonality as possible from one model to the next. To this end, and after the move to Wairakei Rd, personell were not seated according to model but according to circuit block. Hence the "groups" were born, later becoming known as the technology groups. For the T500 series design, a power supply and audio group consisted of Mike Morrin. Mike's father was a skilled auto electrician, apparently well known in vintage car club circles. I was once given the magneto from a 1906 Darracq to give to Mike to give to his father for refurbishment. Almost 40 years later it still runs trouble free. The car can be viewed at the Route 79 Museum, a few km south of Geraldine. The synthesiser group consisted of Han Overtoom and Neil Keller. The receiver group: Mark McKinstry, and me when required. "When required", means shrinking the UHF receiver as outlined in the next chapter and picking up the AM receiver when the first attempt which had been "read across" from an FM design proved to be inadequate. The Transmitter group consisted variously of Terry Collins, Dave Festing, Peter Forth and Trevor Laughton, these personnel shifting around a little. There would always be Terry but often just one or two of the others. Terry was exceptional. Whereas Zverev was never far from Dave Festing, Terry was never far from the "vector voltmeter", a piece of test equipment that had been bought on the recommendation of Ray Vickers along the way. It was hard to use but even harder to convert the readings from its meters into meaningful results. During the time at Manchester Street, there had been a proliferation of components known as "air-wound inductors". These coils of enamel coated copper wire were defined by a diameter and their numbers of turns. But often a part with small diameter and many turns would exactly match another having a large diameter and few turns, leading to an unnecessary duplication of inventory.

Terry methodically measured all combinations of numbers of turns and diameters, stepping up in half millimetre increments, and compiled a table of the sensible ones. Measurements were taken with the vector voltmeter. It was exacting and tedious work but by making it easy for engineers to select these components, Terry's efforts paid huge dividends. In the original Tait AM sets, receive-transmit antenna switching was performed by a relay, the transparent component with blue graphics top centre on the front cover image. As mentioned in an earlier chapter, these components were susceptible to vibration. In the T190s a new technology using components called "pin diodes" was adopted. For the VHF T500 series products, Terry had proposed using a relay again due to the expense of the pin diodes. To add to the fear the relay would not be plugged into a socket, but directly soldered. Any familiar with the AM relay situation were extremely nervous but Terry insisted that a "DC whetting current" would eliminate the vibration problem. In spite of the nervousness, the relay was chosen. Terry was right, it never caused a hint of trouble, not even in the AM version. For this, the T510, Peter Forth had been assigned to the transmitter design. He'd largely finished it before returning to his home country, England. Taking over another's work is always hard. Terry knew all the techniques in transmitter design and by understanding Peter's approach, was able to complete the design exactly as it had been started.

Engineers recorded their design notes and test results in manifold books although I don't remember the carbon copies ever being collected. Some oscilloscopes and spectrum analysers had storage displays that could temporarily hold an image after which a modified Polaroid camera could be used to take an instant photograph of it. Some stuck these into their manifold books, but of course the carbon copy would show nothing. As a step to try better to preserve knowledge through staff turnover, the requirement for design reports was introduced. When a design was complete, theoretical considerations together with calculations were presented along with explanations and test reports. These were beneficial but there were exceptions. When the examiner marks a mathematics paper and sees a correct answer devoid of any working, was it a lucky guess or a genius student? John Croft and Colin McKenzie being highly experienced were able to do immense conceptual work in their heads, after which they could sketch the schematic and design the printed circuit board artwork. After building a prototype, a few component values would be tweaked to result in a solid design of good performance. In cases like this, little more than test results could be included in the design report. But in other cases the design report was a good idea, both for teaching and learning. They also kept management informed, Ray Vickers once talking to me about gain distributions in the T510 (see below) after presumably reading the design report.

One area of cost savings in the receivers related to the crystal filter, an example of such being the very large component left of centre in the front cover photograph. From Drake's Radio Cyclopedia of 1933: *Selectivity is the ability of a receiver to respond to the signals from one transmitting station without being affected by or responding to the signals from other stations of nearly the same frequency as the one being received.* This definition still holds, with selectivity in all the pre T500 Tait fully transistorised sets being provided by crystals filters. For the T500 receivers, a smaller cheaper crystal filter was used in combination with cheaper technology going by the name "ceramic filter". The integrated circuit already in use for the intermediate frequency in the handhelds was easily adapted to this new way of doing things. For the T510, an AM intermediate frequency amplifier was piggybacked onto the integrated circuit and the frontend copied from the VHF set. When results proved to be disappointing, the design was handed over to me, being the only available person with previous AM receiver experience. The chapters on the T152 sets and handhelds give some explanation of the dual conversion superheterodyne principle. For the handhelds and the new T500 receivers, the integrated circuit incorporated the "second mixer", which had been designed for FM, not AM, the latter being more demanding of a receiver's hardware than the former. Some revealing measurements of this second mixer exposed its shortcomings, after which a remedy was devised. Existing receiver design philosophy, as had been introduced by Dennis Chapman, had placed rules on a facet of receiver design known as "gain distribution" and the first "read across" T510 design had obeyed these as they had applied to FM. There was never any doubt that these rules were valid, but when the inadequacies of the second mixer were factored in, the rules had to be optimised differently. When the frontend was redesigned accordingly, the T510 receiver performed well.

The planning of projects, followed by their day to day management was usually the domain of the engineering managers, Joe Fone's cartoon in an earlier chapter showing the magnitude of the situation. A management decision was taken to shift some of the project management load onto the more experienced of the design engineers. Of the assignable numbers of the T500 series, T510, T530 and T550 were taken. T520 had been reserved for low band VHF and T540 for Band 3, the VHF frequencies around 200MHz which were being vacated by television as this transitioned to UHF. As the first three T500s were coming to fruition, the go ahead was given for the T520, with the short straw for its project management being drawn by me, who would also design the receiver, as this entailed no more than the design of a new frontend, the remainder of the receiver being in common with the T530 and T550. Neil Keller from the synthesiser group designed the new voltage controlled oscillator circuitry, or VCO. By this time, VCO design required a very high level of skill and experience, not only for the electronic design, but also because these oscillators had a tendency to be vibration sensitive. For the original AM sets, the relays had been problematic in this respect, now it was the turn of the VCO. On one of his trips to the Tait UK office, Angus had found a secondhand Ling Vibration Table and so paid the money and had it freighted home. When it arrived it was set up in the production area as specialist staff there had exactly the right skillset for operating and maintaining equipment of this nature. The mechanism under the horizontal table was a giant version of the voice coil in a loudspeaker, more than a foot in diameter. At a later date, this did actually shake itself apart. The production engineering staff wound a new coil on their lathe and sealed it with epoxy. I remember being very impressed with the high standard of workmanship. This instrument, which allowed for both the acceleration and frequency of vibration to be adjusted, became one very useful analysis tool. Another was something that Doug McConnell invented at home during one of his many flashes of genius. Telephone earpieces of the day worked on a principle called "balanced armature". Doug removed the diaphragm from an old one of these and soldered a 50 millimetre wire stalk in its place. When the device was connected to an audio oscillator and the stalk brought into contact with the various components of the VCO, the vulnerability of each could be determined. It was tedious work but helped lead to a result.

For the transmitter there was no hope of any progress because this was one of those times when the head count in the transmitter group was just two, Trevor Laughton and Terry Collins. Peter Forth had returned to England and Dave Festing was enjoying a new lifestyle on a few acres out at Oxford. It was anticipated that Terry would take up the T520 once finished his current assignment, a task projected to take some months. In one of my rare but cherished meetings with Angus, I was asked for suggestions. Stuck for something to say I mentioned Dave Festing, never imagining it could happen and thinking nothing more of it. Next morning Terry had something to share. He said he'd had a call from Dave Festing with news that Angus had just offered him a job. At hearing this, I was as shocked as Terry was. Dave began on the T520 transmitter soon after, progressing well. After Dave, Neil and I had completed the designs for our own sections, they were put together for the first time within the first complete prototype of the T520. In the space of time that personnel had been organised into technology groups, the level of knowledge within each group had flourished. However this came at the expense of knowledge of what might happen when the circuit blocks offered up by the groups were paired together. With this lack of knowledge, came a hiccup. Transmitter power-up caused the voltage controlled oscillator to momentarily change frequency, a highly undesirable situation. The standard technique for solving an interaction of this nature involved the addition of a buffer. I was in the hot seat and by designing a buffer circuit that meshed with the existing printed circuit board layout and then modifying the artwork myself, was able to solve this problem.

From the very beginnings of the "cheapie", it hadn't escaped anyone's notice that its proposed plastic enclosure would be transparent to radio frequencies and that many components, wires and copper traces of the circuitboard would act as antennae. By this time official standards had appeared that placed strict limits of how much radio interference was allowed to leak from a radiotelephone's enclosure. At the time, such leaking signals were known as cabinet radiations or "cab rads", for short. Given so many potential radiating sources within the product, some form of shielding was required and there were two likely contenders, tinplate shields or spray-on conductive coatings. The latter initially sounded attractive but proved to be impractical for a number of reasons. Tinplate had the advantage that integrated leaf spring elements, known as "floopers" in Tait-speak, would make reliable contact with the printed circuit board and other shielding. Creating effective shielding was hardest at UHF and got progressively easier with reducing frequency. When I mentioned to Angus that the low band VHF T520 had passed cab rads, he was complimentary but tempered the achievement with some reality, "…of course, a cynic would say, you can almost hear it down there!" meaning that the frequencies involved were closer to audio than to UHF.

All the while the mechanical design progressed smoothly. It had been anticipated that the Christchurch company PDL would be the supplier of all the injection moulded parts. Initially PDL had rebuffed the opportunity, explaining that they did not have the available resources due to their other commitments. But after discussions at the very highest level, a supply agreement was reached. When the first prototype samples appeared, they didn't look good at all with blemishes, sink holes and missing detail.

Gordon Todd seemed to be the one most familiar with how the injection moulding process developed from the first off-tool samples through to production and was able to explain that perfection was easily within reach. And it was. The finished article was easy on the eye, but Steve knew how to make it even better by seeking the involvement of a graphic artist.

T500. Red indicator LEDs shine through printed red lens. Microphone cable bottom centre.

Beauty is in the eye of the beholder and many beholders concurred on the fine looks of the T500. A whizzy promotional video added what looked like animated computer graphics reminiscent of Star Wars. It was a good product and in a short space of time was good for the company's books.

After the manufacturing arm had moved to Wairakei Rd, the roadmap to automation continued. Automatic insertion machines were purchased. In these machines, goose-bill jaws accurately gripped a component's leads, after which a table accurately moved the printed circuit board until that component's destination point was positioned exactly below the jaws. The component was then pushed fully home after which an underside operation cut and bent the leads just enough to prevent the component from falling out again. Not all components could be auto-inserted, but the majority could. A "D-List" of the components available for auto-insertion was circulated around the company. From memory there were about 80 and the selection included the most used resistors, capacitors and transistors. When designing new products engineers would try to design circuits around the D-List components. By the mid-80s, automated equipment for electronic manufacturing was beginning to revolve around the IBM personal computer and many personnel in manufacturing roles became superusers of these. In a twist of irony, these auto-insertion machines could load components into the T190s and even the yet older AM sets, but not into the latest T500, due to components having been fitted vertically. At this time, printed circuit board hole spacing for resistors had been 10.16 millimetres. A new kind of resistor, using a technology named "metal film", offered smaller resistors that fitted holes spaced at 5.08 millimetres. When the T500 printed circuit boards were redesigned on the new CAD system to accept these new resistors together with other components from the "D-List" this product moved into the new age of auto-insertion. It was rebranded the T500 Series II and included other advancements relating to the mechanical assembly. Performance was identical to the original.

One facet of the T500 that had contributed to its value for money was a very limited palette of options. For example there was a limit of just two channels. It had been aimed at the bulk of the market. A multichannel version of the same design was proposed and named the T600. Design work, including the addition of a channel switch, did begin but the whole project was cancelled before it neared production. A T700 project had commenced too, the thinking being that this product would cater for the "luxury" end of the market while the T500, together with the later and identical looking T500 Series II, would fill the bread-and-butter end. Han Overtoom led the T700. It was a "do everything design" having chassis and covers of diecast aluminium. To demonstrate its ruggedness, a photograph was taken of it under the front wheel of a Mack or Kenworth truck. Apart from a minor depression in the diecast top cover, the experiment had caused no damage. Rubber sealing of the covers allowed other photographs to show a T700 being sprayed with water, while under these covers, significant space had been allocated for a variety of optional ancillary circuitboards. As the number sequence might suggest, there was a T800 in the mix.

The first all transistorised receivers and transmitters for use in repeater systems had been adaptations of the AM sets. The first FM repeater units were split out of the T193 on Charles Dickey's kitchen table as described in an earlier chapter. Then in the late 70s, design for a new and improved lineup of basestation products commenced, Doug McConnell being the manager. Doug had previously worked at Philips New Zealand and I once remember him describing some of their design philosophies. For example, designers were not confined to use only Philips components. Where a competitor component was better, the Philips part would then languish whereupon the Philips division making that part would respond by making a superior one. Doug's design work at Tait had included some tone call equipment. A 3-Tone unit could be used for signalling over a radio channel. These were nice to set up and never went wrong. For FM radiotelephones an emerging technology was CTCSS or, Continuous Tone Coded Squelch Systems. When the T196 etc were initially conceived it was envisaged that there would be long sets and short sets, the former having room at the front for a CTCSS circuitboard. Doug nutted out a digital filtering system for this which he was able to implement in hardware. These units were easy to set up and again, never went wrong. Meanwhile an American company marketed a tiny CTCSS module based on an analogue technique called "state-variable". These units were fiddly and a little time consuming to set up but did the job. Because they were tiny, they could be fitted into short sets, allowing long sets to be deleted from the Tait catalogue, thereby reducing inventory. Later again, the CTCSS function would be executed in software. Among the products being designed by Doug's group was a new AM receiver. This was a clean slate design being undertaken by an engineer from the UK, Mike Fitch.

A home constructor article for a 20 Watt stereo amplifier published in the May 1972 edition of Practical Wireless magazine begins, "It is an unwritten law of electronics that whenever a group of engineers are gathered together, then sooner or later a HiFi amplifier will be designed." Among the staff in their twenties and early thirties, I don't remember any

Ham Radio operators. There was however a keen interest in audio amplifiers. Dennis Chapman had designed an amplifier based on the "current dumping" philosophy. Mark Empson also had a keen interest in amplifier design and together with a business partner founded Aucom. Although beginning with audio as the name suggests, the company ventured into starters for industrial electric motors and still flourishes today. Mike Fitch had built valve amplifiers for rock bands in the UK using the famous KT88 beam tetrodes in the output. For the new AM receiver, Mike was exploring ways of bettering the receivers of the AM sets. As mentioned in other chapters, as well as having good sensitivity, the ability to receive distant weak signals, a receiver must also have the ability to reject unwanted signals. One susceptibility of receivers to unwanted signals that is difficult to counteract, is known as "intermodulation". Colin McKenzie once explained to me that the New Zealand Post Office had initially set the requirement for intermodulation at 60 decibels but later reduced it to 57 after a consensus of New Zealand manufacturers protested that 60 was unachievable. Colin went on to explain that in quite short order, Tait receivers had achieved 60 decibels after all. After a detailed analysis together with some new design ideas, Mike was able to eke out a few more decibels, but along at way he said to me, "It just shows how good the original Tait AM receiver is."

By the mid to late 80s, the time had come to bring the basestation product lines up to the ultimate level of performance, the next number, T800 being assigned to the series. Neil Keller took the helm for this entire project. The objective was to make the products the best it was possible to make them. Whereas the T700 had had a diecast chassis that a few circuitboards dropped into, the T800s would have a single printed circuit board that was sandwiched between an upper chassis and an underside cover. In addition the upper chassis would have a removable top cover, resulting in a design having easy access to both sides of the printed circuit board. Joins were designed in such a way as to block the path of any errant radio signals, resulting in good sealing against cabinet radiation. By this time, manufacturing had invested heavily in a surface mount assembly line. Rather than components with wires that fitted through holes and soldered to the bottom side of the printed circuit board, surface mounted components had no wire leads and soldered directly to pads on the topside. The small dimensions of the components suited radio work eminently and the topside placement was a boon to automated assembly. As one final bonus, the end product would look extremely neat. One of the sales managers from England expressed this in the following way. He said when he visited any of the many UK dealers with a sample T800 product for their perusal, he would present their senior technician with the product, a screwdriver and a box of tissues and then stand back and watch. The technician would whiz through the self-explanatory dismantling whereupon he would be so awed with the beauty of the interior that uncontrollable salivating would make the tissues essential. It was always interesting to hear an imaginative sales pitch.

This was 1990 and during the same talk, this sales manager spoke of the aggressive cell phone sales tactics in the UK. He referenced one mail order company that offered free phones, on a plan of course, with a 20 pound cash back. The customer would receive the phone, all ready to go, in the mail complete with an invoice for nothing that had a twenty pound note stapled to it. The manager's talk was all about stressing the need for a new Tait handheld model. By this time the T302, T303 and T307 had reached obsolescence. Another interesting sales pitch had surrounded these products a few years earlier. This Tait product in its thick leather case, although large and heavy, was extremely robust. In some countries it was said, this was seen as an advantage by law enforcement. Use of the truncheon often had to be followed by a detailed written report at the station whereas a gentle biff from a rugged handheld could often defuse escalating aggression but not attract the burden of pen and paper at the end of the day. In the mid 80s, a new handheld project did in fact commence but was cancelled. Whether it is light rail, a stadium or a roading project, there are always cost and time blowouts. The new handheld project did not even get far enough along to suffer blowouts. But the T500 project had suffered delays making it reasonable to assume that the new handheld would too. Engineering resources were finite and company finances were tightening, making it sensible to direct engineering resources into products that would pay the best dividends. In the memo that announced the decision to close down the handheld project, Angus made reference to the words of General MacArthur, without quoting what they were. The famous words were of course "I shall return". These words were bannered by the media after being picked from a speech given by the general in Australia. MacArthur did indeed return to the Philippines. Equally, a Tait handheld did return as the T3000, but I had long departed the company by then. After cancellation of the handheld project and as the T500 Series II project came to an end, as many engineering resources as possible were mustered up and directed into the T2000 project.

I Shall Return. The monument photographed in 2003 depicts MacArthur's steps through the surf from a landing craft after his forces arrived at Leyte, Philippines, October 1944.

A Magic Track Pin

The first Tait UHF set (ultra high frequency) was known as the T196. It operated at frequencies in the range of 400 to 520MHz (Mega Hertz). In UHF receivers of the day, instead of tuned circuits employing inductors and capacitors, Helical Resonators were used. While very effective and reliable, these had the disadvantage of being tedious and expensive to reproduce. When adjustable, or trimmer, capacitors with teflon dielectric became available, the way was at last clear for traditional tuned circuits to be used in the frontends of compact UHF receivers. The engineer who proposed the idea conducted a feasibility study and found the components to be suitable. The next step, carried out by a subordinate, involved the construction and testing of a complete UHF frontend. Once proven, the concept was earmarked for use in a future generation of Tait product that would become known as the T500 series. But as the T500 concept fell into place, it became apparent that the area allocated to the receiver frontend was insufficient to accommodate the prototype circuit described above. To make matters worse, the person familiar with the design had vacated the company by this time. So the task of making it fit fell to a third individual, me. In radio receiver design there is always the risk that some of the output of a circuit might find its way to the input of the same circuit and recirculate, the higher the frequency, the higher the likelihood. For the T500 UHF set, the decision was taken early on to put tinplate shielding around the receiver frontend as a first defence against any recirculation. This more than anything else allowed the design to be shrunk.

Before the late 80s, import restrictions were such that it was easier to go with NZ suppliers even if they lagged a little behind overseas offerings in terms of the latest developments. A case in point was printed circuit boards

(PCBs). In the 60s, 70s and 80s, most PCB makers supported the NZ radio and television industries, where most circuit boards had required copper on one side only. Concurrently, overseas suppliers offered multilayer boards where layers were interconnected via copper plated holes. Multilayer boards were never available from Christchurch suppliers and for dual layer boards, copper plated "vias" became available only after the mid-80s. From the 70s, dual layer boards were available but connections between the top and bottom copper layers had to be made with dedicated components, fitted during electronic assembly. These were known as track pins. They looked like large sewing pins, but only 3mm long. After fitting, the heads were soldered to the top of the PCB with a soldering iron. The bottom ends were left to be soldered during the wave soldering process along with all the other component leads.

Throughout the history of radio design, secure grounding or earthing within circuits has been essential. Where double sided PCB is used, one reliable technique is to reserve the entire top copper layer for earthing. Especially when working at UHF, some of the bottom copper layer might also be relegated to earth. In this case, the top and bottom earth layers would normally be "stitched" together with ample numbers of copper plated vias or, in the absence of copper plated holes, connected together with track pins while bearing in mind that the manual fitting process placed limits on the numbers that could be used. When tinplate shielding is fitted to a circuit board, in addition to the obvious shielding function, earthing is improved. Even so, when compared to plated through PCBs, tinplate shielding in combination with track pins is a second best solution. However, by the early 80s the Tait engineering lab was well endowed with test equipment. Fine signal generators, spectrum analysers, modulation meters, a vector voltmeter and the usual storage oscilloscopes and meters. In contrast to this abundance, 40 years earlier when Angus Tait had worked on airborne radar in the UK, the most sophisticated piece of test equipment had been a basic oscilloscope.

The first step to fitting the UHF frontend into the allocated space was to produce a circuitboard layout. This was in the days before CAD and so correspondence between schematic and layout had to be thoroughly checked manually. Layouts were usually drawn double sized in pencil and on graph paper from where they were transcribed into artworks composed of Bishop Graphics tapes. In order for the frontend to fit in the allocated area, spacings between components and between connections had to be reduced to a bare minimum. There was some initial concern when composing the artwork that the design might be too tight, but it turned out to be within the capabilities of manufacturing. When the first prototypes were tested, results were good. Receiver sensitivity had not been adversely affected by the shrink and the closer proximity of inputs to outputs had not invited any unwanted recirculation. However, there is very much more to receiver design than sensitivity to the wanted signal. There are multitudes of unwanted signals that a receiver must reject. Much of the required rejection is provided by the tuned circuits in the frontend. Fortunately the shrink did not adversely affect the ability of the tuned circuits to reject unwanted signals although their properties did change. A "notch" appeared near the region of the "image frequency", being the most prominent of the unwanted signal frequencies. In this context, "notch" refers to a small band of frequencies whose passage is severely restricted. To be exploited, the position of the notch would have to be moved relative to the wanted signal, so that it would block the passage of unwanted signals at the image frequency.

For the notch to be moved, the mechanism causing it would need to be understood. As hinted at above, the cause related to the security of the grounding or lack thereof. The rudimentary circuit simulation available to Taits in the day was of little help here as it did not have the ability to resolve a physical ground plane and/or chassis into point to point circuit values. Dealing with the vagaries of RF design had always been a major strength at Tait. One of the tools used was the “wand”. This was no more than 50mm of 3mm plastic tube supporting a small piece of ferrite at one end and a small piece of brass at the other. When approached by the ferrite, the inductance of a conductor would be increased due to the permeability of the ferrite. When approached by the brass, inductance would be reduced due to the perimeter of the brass slug acting as a shorted turn. This simple tool could be used to quickly build up a mental picture of the sensitivity of various conductors to inductance change and, to some extent, variation in earthing inductance. After enough such hints, a direct assault was made on the earthing. Due to the unavailability of plated through vias, ideal earthing could not be contemplated. But by removing and refitting various of the track pins, the relative importance of each could be investigated. For most, the effect was small. But for one in particular, the effect was dramatic. After this discovery, a miniature hacksaw blade was ground down to make a tiny hole saw. With this, the hole of the sensitive track pin was slotted so that the position of it could be moved. After a little trial and error a position was found for the track pin that resulted in the notch falling on the image frequency. Moreover, as the frontend was tuned over the UHF band, the notch tracked in such a way that it always provided sufficient rejection at the image frequency. In a salute to serendipity, it became known as "the magic track pin". At this time, tracking notches were already used in some Tait VHF receiver designs where the technique usually involved the addition of a capacitor or inductor. But in this case, the tracking notch was had for nothing. That is, less-than secure earthing of the ground plane and/or chassis was taking the place of the added inductor. A later addition to the engineering staff who had not been involved in the design arbitrarily contended that the chassis should not be used as a component. But the established wisdom was practicality. Simply put, a design must be fully reproducible under all circumstances. This design was. The position of the track pin was permanently set in the second prototype. The tracking notch behaved exactly as before, as it continued to do throughout subsequent prototypes and production. Plated-through printed circuit boards became available in Christchurch from the late 1980's. A Series II version of the T500 (T5x5) using this technology was developed. Rather than trying to exploit copper plated vias for more secure earthing, the expedient approach of simply replacing track pins with vias was taken. This way, the designs could be expected to perform exactly as before. And so they did. The tracking notch behaved identically. But in spite of the successful design, the T500 UHF receiver did have some teething troubles.

The design's reason for being was the teflon trimmer capacitors and the examples of these used throughout initial development were well made. But after production had ramped up, the examples supplied in volume were not always immune to vibration with the result that some receivers would fall out of alignment after sustained use in harsh vehicle environments. By this time, a suitable ceramic trimmer capacitor had become available. For the teflon components, the adjustment screw was at the "earthy" potential. But for the new ceramic components the adjustment was at the "hot" potential. At this time, trim tools had shafts of plastic that held a metal blade at each end. Although the metal blade measured only a few square millimetres in area, when contacting the "hot" adjustment screw of the ceramic trimmer, the minuscule added capacitance was sufficient to disturb the tuning point. This left the ceramic trimmers in the position of being ideal components that were impossible to tune. The solution came from the product support group. Staff there discovered a trim tool with ceramic blade. These trim tools had negligible affect when in contact with a trimmer's adjustment screw allowing production to change to the ceramic trimmers, ending all vibration problems.

The Thousands for the Nineties

Water finds its own level and if the move to direct engineers into project management had been some kind of experiment, the results were highly informative to say the least. Neil Keller and Trevor Laughton, both excellent design engineers, proved to be stellar in project management positions. From there, both advanced into senior leadership roles within the company. Again, if it had been an experiment, the results had impinged on engineering management too. But even before this, the responsibilities of John Croft in the handheld group had diminished as the T303, T302 and T307 had all come to fruition. A product support group had been set up so that when any product developed a hiccup during production, product support would be the first responder, thereby removing any distraction from the design engineers. John Croft took up the leadership position of this group, leaving just Ray Vickers and Doug McConnell managing engineering proper, neither now having serious project management responsibilities. After 1985, job opportunities were opening up at Dennis Chapman's company, Eltec. Andrew Davidson, Peter May and Simon Sloan were the first to move across. After Lester Parkes' successful application there, Ray Vickers was appointed to the type approval roll that Lester had vacated. When I joined Tait Electronics in 1976, there had been a lone engineering manager, Denis Cottle from memory. Now without the burden of project management it could be a one person job again and Doug McConnell was appointed to the position, although he soon found he needed an administrative assistant.

By the late 80s the mechanical, transmitter, receiver, synthesiser and audio/power groups had accumulated high levels of knowledge and experience, Keith Lewis, Mark Siddell and Steve Pastoll having been added to the synthesiser group after Han and Neil moved on. In addition there was now a digital group charged with the incorporation of microprocessor technology into Tait products. Neil's basestation projects were ticking over nicely. The cancelled T600 and handheld projects were out of everyone's minds and Trevor Laughton had managed the T500 Series II project very efficiently. It made sense that Trev would therefore head a new mobile project. Perhaps the T900 number had been available, but the marketing people wanted to be a little more futuristic and T1000 must have seemed too close to the hundreds. The approaching new millennium was just too tempting and T2000 was the number chosen. Trev did more than merely lead the design. He led the concept. He gathered together Sally Anne Frazer from marketing as the interface to the customer, Ian Crawley as the mechanical designer and me to keep tabs on how the circuit blocks from the technology groups would go together. There were meetings with various customers and service departments. In one such meeting I was particularly interested in what Norm Clark from Christchurch Branch had to offer. Since the T152, Tait had always recommended that radiotelephones be left turned on overnight and throughout weekends as this way an employee would not miss a call by forgetting to switch it on. The Tait synthesised sets drew more current and Norm mentioned that some customers were beginning to have Monday morning starting troubles. Norm went on to explain that the higher current was fine on a new battery, but if the T2000 was to be even more extravagant on current than the T490s, customers would end up having to replace their car batteries more often than before. It would not be a show stopper but the example illustrates the level of detail we got down to for the design brief.

Another interesting idea related to "customer". For sure, the end customer would be the taxi driver or police officer etc. But if the product could appear super attractive to the dealers, then enthusiastic dealers would take it to the customers. The idea was not new. Through the 1950s Britain had been the motorcycle capital of the world. All the dealers were highly loyal to the English marques. The Japanese manufacturers approached the dealers with low cubic-centimetre models which didn't compete against the English models because these were generally of higher capacity. The

A T2000 Prototype imaged on an Epson 1240U scanner. The irregular shaped piece at top left, covers the main printed circuit board except for the two areas with the ribbon looms. The control board then swings over and mounts on the cover. Top and bottom covers, with lugs that hold the front panel in place, complete the assembly.

dealers could sign up contracts for these small Japanese models while retaining dealerships for their English flagships. The dealers then learned a very quick lesson. The Japanese machines were reliable, performed well, didn't leak oil and were needless of warranty repair. Altogether, they were easier to make money from than the British models. So in a few years' time when the Japanese offered larger cc models that competed directly with the British marques, the dealers were left with no choice but to choose the practical cashflow route against old loyalties. By "selling" to the dealers, in addition to all their other marketing efforts, the Japanese conquered the motorcycle industry in a dozen years. Our motive was not so cutthroat, but it seemed like a good idea to make the dealer's life as easy as possible. Tait speak for a convenient radiotelephone became "supermarket radio". The days of the dealer having to do a final run up would be gone. Instead, the T2000 would be configured by a laptop computer, via a cable temporarily plugged in place of the microphone. Installation in the customer's vehicle would still be required of course, but the supermarket radio concept would be a good bonus for the dealer.

The T2000 concept took the best of what Tait Electronics had done to date. The beauty of the T800, the functionality of the T700 and the simplicity of the T500 were all rolled up into one. But whereas the T500 had been enclosed in plastic, the workings of the T2000 would have an all diecast aluminium enclosure with just the front module, or control head, being made from plastic. There were two choices for the front module, basic and advanced. The functionality of the basic matched the T500 but with the addition of an internal forward facing loudspeaker. Instead of a loudspeaker, the advanced module had a telephone style keypad and alphanumeric LCD display. Either front module could be attached directly to the T2000 or be connected to it via a long cable. As car interiors filled with centre consoles and other embellishments, this meant that the compact control module could be dash mounted and the T2000 unit installed under a seat or in the rear luggage space. All of this thinking brought into focus how the T2000 would appear from the outside. All the

A very original Tait "made in New Zealand" speaker and replacement 5x3 driver unit. The later New Zealand made speakers featured a centre Tait logo. The complete speaker unit for the T2000, bottom right, was sourced off shore.

while, the internal layout was being fleshed out. This was the heyday of the technology groups. In fact all groups were staffed with high grade people and all circuits were being designed with the new surface mounted components which were much better suited to the VHF and UHF bands than the previous leaded components had been. This wasn't all positive however, with one in particular of the new whiz kids using the superiority of modern advances for reason to disparage some of the old designs, even once making a parody of Tennyson's poem about the Charge of the Light Brigade but, in the first line, changing 600 to 500 and pinning this to a noticeboard. Clever perhaps, but short sighted. Sales of the T500 were paying his wages. There could be no doubt that the circuit designs from the technology groups were the best that could be designed. They simply were.

As the designs by the groups were kicking off, thought was being given to how they would go together and how the T2000 as a whole would perform. As the externally driven concepts had firmed up and the internally driven requirement for shielding walls had come to a consensus, Ian Crawley had commenced the mechanical design on the CAD system. Ian was a Dassault CATIA user par excellence. By this time there were too many in all the groups to remember the names of but Dave Mason, one of the longer standing of the mechanical group and knowing the dos and don'ts of aluminium diecasting, made sure that the design that would eventually fall from the CAD would be manufacturable. Trev organised the project so that as many things as possible could happen at the same time. As mentioned elsewhere, this is an obvious concept going by the buzzword "parallel design", but how to make it happen isn't always so obvious. As the mechanical design got close, samples of the various pieces were sourced from sub-contractors who milled them from solid aluminium. These would be valuable to the suppliers who would eventually make the diecasting tools. But more so, they could be used for advanced testing of the one aspect that usually had to wait until last; cab-rads. But why? And how can cab-rads leak through aluminium anyway? The answer is: They don't. They leak through joins and cable entry points. Joins were not expected to leak because tongue and groove sealing techniques had been built into the chassis and covers. The main offenders were expected to be cables, such as those for DC power and external loudspeaker, because they act as antennae. The normal solution to this was always to add filter capacitors at the cable entry points, these points usually being on the main connector. However, because this usually involved tricky hand assembly, a new approach was sought for the T2000.

From the outset it was envisaged that the main printed circuit board would be divided into compartments by shielding walls built into the chassis. If the compartment that hosted the main connector had no radio energy, then the main connector would not need the difficult-to-fit filter capacitors. Instead it would be necessary to prevent radio energy from entering this compartment and this could be easily achieved with machine placed surface mounted capacitors. This was not the only new idea that passing cab-rads depended on. With upfront cab-rad testing all the new ideas could be verified in advance. But how? A Complete T2000 design was many many months away still. The answer was to rehash a complete T500 UHF set, the T550, to fit into the T2000 chassis. This meant no less than a complete re-layout to the T550 onto a printed circuit board of the T2000 shape. Some were horrified by the idea, as if it might somehow destine the T2000 to Tennyson's valley of death. But it was done and all the ideas that were to be verified were tested and improved as necessary. A year or so later and after I had departed Tait Electronics, Trev phoned me to advise that the T2000 had passed cab-rads after the addition of just one component.

As previously mentioned, the output from the technology groups always excelled. But projects always took longer to complete than had been projected. In the past, projects that needed just one or two people, had been completed in a year. But it seemed the more people the longer the time. The early parts of projects such as getting to a first prototype would generally go smoothly. But as time progressed it would be discovered that one aspect of a design had painted another aspect into a corner. Interaction problems appeared that were reminiscent of the farmer with the wheat, chicken and fox crossing the river pair by pair except that a decision agreed by all a month ago had changed the diet of the chicken. Engineering projects are hard. Try to think of an engineering infrastructure project that came in under the initial time and budget estimates? I remember one of the marketing personnel talking to me about how he had observed that morale would fade three quarters of the way through a project. Doug McConnell often mentioned the 80 20 rule and how the first 20% of the effort gave 80% of the result after which it took 80% more effort to get the last 20% of the result. It was John Croft's poster exactly, except that with time, confusion blurred into despondency. In military doctrine, discipline and morale go together and in there somewhere must be determination. This highlights the major disadvantage of technology groups. It's hard to form a cohesive and determined project group from individuals that are out of earshot of each other. I remember much discussion of this with Doug and other senior people in the lab. There just didn't seem to be a way to keep the technology groups at their acme and still have cohesive project groups. After I had left I heard that the focus had shifted toward project groups with the technology groups eventually being condensed into one single group that covered all the technologies and was overseen by Keith Lewis. Keith had joined the company when the T500 design was coming to a close and took up a position as leader of the synthesiser group where he made significant improvements to the technology.

When manufacturing had first moved to 30 Manchester Street, the lab was on the first floor of a High St premises. This was actually my first contact with Tait Electronics as I had a job interview there with Mr Cottle, the engineering manager. Unsure of the way in, I ascended outside stairs which turned out to be the fire escape, but someone let me in and ushered me to the boss' office. The manufacturing people sometimes lightheartedly voiced a view that engineer's designs advanced to "she'll be right" status and were then "thrown over the wall" to the factory. This was one example of "many a true word spoken in jest". But it didn't happen through any form of neglect. Semiconductor devices for VHF were still leading edge when I began in 1976, particularly the mosfets used in the receiver frontends. The manufacturers of these parts could not avoid inconsistency

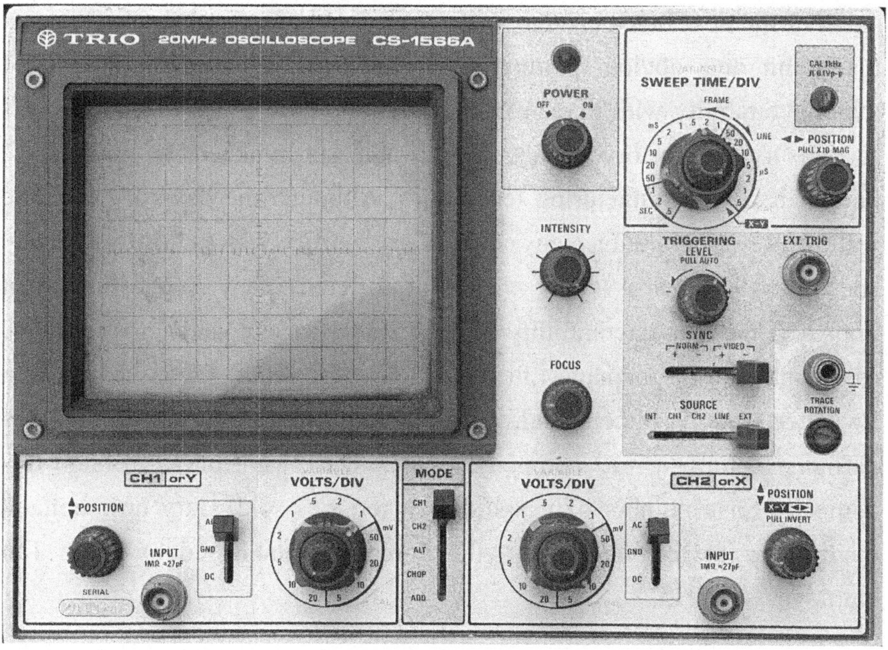

Trio test equipment was good value for money and a staple of oscilloscopes, AC Voltmeters and signal generators at Tait in the 1980s. Trio rebranded as Kenwood through the 80s and merged with JVC in 2008. A decade later, JVC Kenwood bought into the Tait organisation. Not quite yet an Admirable Crichton situation...

between batches and it was not possible for Tait engineers to anticipate how the next batch might behave. Inevitably a first sign of trouble would be discovered by a run-up technician. "Instability" was the technical term for the usual problem. Technicians were often home constructors and soon, one would devise a fix, usually in the form of a capacitor added to the back of the circuitboard. This would be documented and the component added during assembly. In another month or two the process might repeat, with a second capacitor added to fix the latest instability. After the second or third capacitor, an engineer would be assigned to appraise the situation and find the core of the problem. In addition to the batch to batch variation, performance of these semiconductors was improving and along with that, their propensity for instability. The engineering solution would usually involve a much simpler fix, only for the cycle of modifications to begin again at the next batch change. Gary Foot had begun in manufacturing in his youth and obviously must have followed all aspects relating to manufacturability with a keen interest. By the time of the T2000, he was second to the factory manager and had accumulated an impressive knowledge of manufacturing techniques. Although the days of "over the wall" had been gone for many years, Gary's office was a short walk away and over the course many visits, he offered many suggestions that improved the manufacturability of the T2000. Gary moved across to Eltec as manufacturing manager in the early 90s. After Eltec changed to Swichtec and was then sold, Gary joined Dennis and other business partners to form a new company, Enatel. Gary went on to manage this company for a number of years until it too was sold. Gary now holds a controlling interest in Salcom, the company established by three Tait employees in 1975.

In the centre hub of the circular saw building at the very top was the staff cafeteria. Sometime in 1990 during a lunch break conversation, a younger engineer devised a plan on how to test drive a Ferrari. Pedal to a dealer on a borrowed 10-speed bike and offer to leave it in his custody while you test drove a basic hatchback. Drive this to the Honda dealer and leave it there while test driving a Honda. Then to the BMW, Mercedes, Porsche and finally, Ferrari. As all heads smiled and nodded in appreciation, one dissenter said "…or you could just walk into the Ferrari Dealer wearing shorts and jandals." This attracted the kind of laughter that only fair play can attract. The comment referred to Dennis Chapman in his customary attire, by then part of Tait folklore. Together with business partners he had founded Eltec in 1985 and owned his first Ferrari half a decade later. While it may have appeared that Dennis was skimming the cream off the Tait crop, such was not the case. When I began at Eltec beginning 1991, I was surrounded by strangers. Only a few had come from Taits. More than that, Eltec were thinking ahead and one table in the cafeteria always stood out. The one seating half a dozen or more trainees. Fifteen years earlier, I had been there at Tait Electronics.

Product Photographs

T152 circa 1970. Note the protruding knobs.

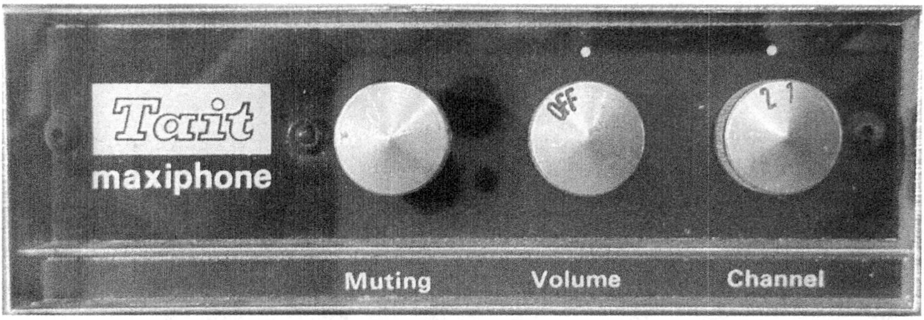

T182. By the mid 70s, all products used these flat knobs.

This plastic front panel was first used on the T193 of late 1976. It went on to be used on all Tait mobile products by the late 1970s in keeping with the mood of car interiors eliminating unnecessary protrusions or abrupt edges.

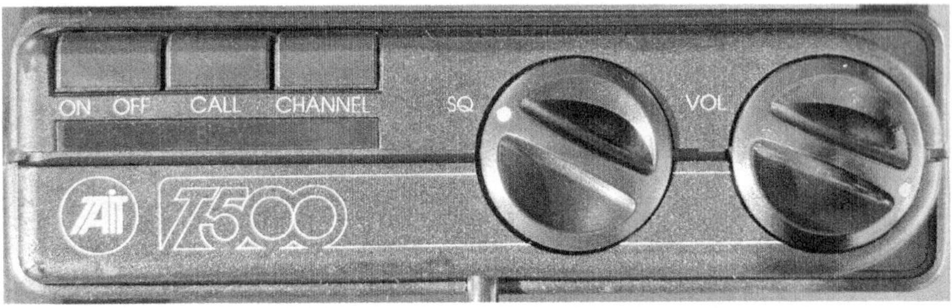

T500. Red indicator LEDs shine through printed red lens at left.
Microphone cable bottom centre.

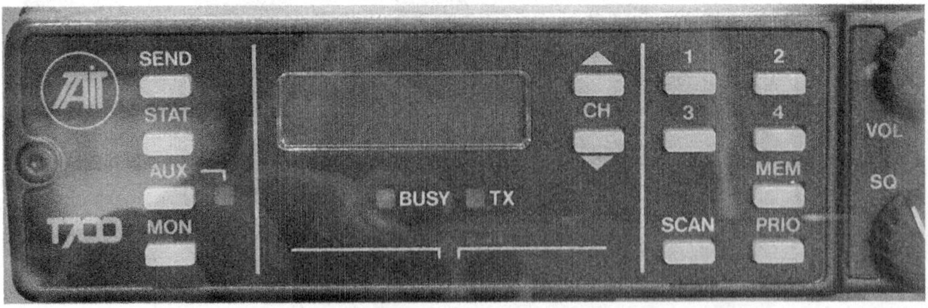

T700 featuring rugged die-cast aluminium front panel.

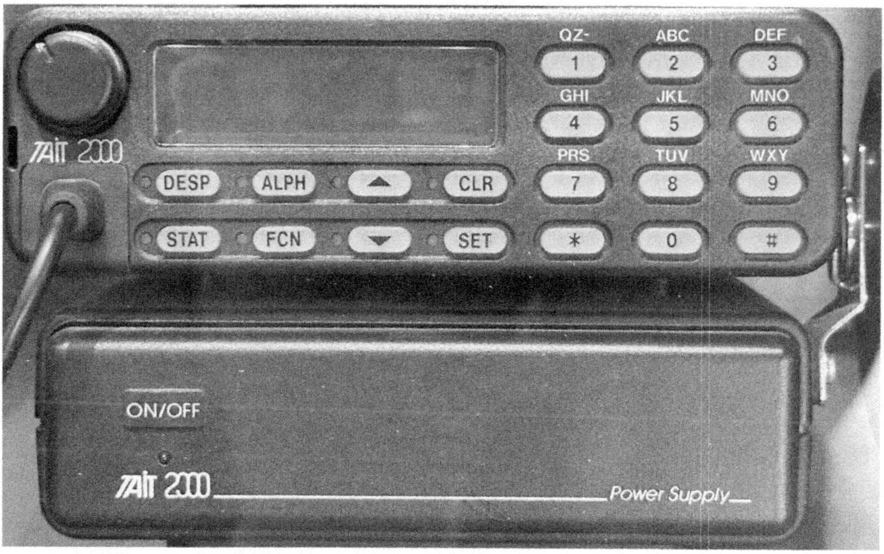

The T508 power supply reused for the T2000 product range. Microphone hook at right

A late model product on display at the Tait Museum. Sports shoe inspired styling appears to have overtaken the "form follows function" look of the original Tait all transistorised models.

Made in the USA
Monee, IL
04 November 2026

67375783R00089